CRAVE ADVANCED PRAISE

"An absolutely fabulous book. 1 action oriented. Ideal for anyone looking to build upon the strengths of their people, leading to more employee engagement and better customer experiences."

> —Colleen Wegman, President and Chief Executive Officer, Wegmans Food Markets

"Once I started *CRAVE*, I couldn't put it down. Gregg Lederman provides the habit-building process to help you build your business. I immediately put the 10 Minutes by Friday method to work for me."

> —Bryan Everett, Chief Operating Officer, Rite Aid Corporation

"Gregg Lederman has written another outstanding book! *CRAVE* will help you think differently about how to behave at work. It's an ideal read for anyone who wants to become a better leader."

> —Mark S. Ain, Founder, Kronos Incorporated

"No fluff here. A science-backed method to positively changing behaviors in an organization. *CRAVE* is a simple read, which means more managers will embrace it and make real change happen."

> —Christopher C. Booth, Chief Executive Officer, Excellus BlueCross BlueShield

San Diego Christian College
Library
Santee, CA

"*CRAVE* is a handbook for all company leaders who want to become more profitable by building a culture of recognition and appreciation. As in most industries, turnover is a significant cost driver in the restaurant business. Lederman shares a simple, habit-building approach to shutting the revolving door by inspiring employees with the WHY, instead of constantly having to tell them WHAT to do."

—Rob Lynch, President, Arby's Restaurant Group, Inc.

"A simple read that goes beyond opinions on the power of employee recognition. Lederman provides the research and biological science to prove it."

—Dr. Jeffrey Peters, Chief Operating Officer,
University Hospitals Health System

"In *CRAVE*, you will learn the key to motivation at work, which is to accept that your job as a leader is not to motivate others. Instead ... you must create the environment that inspires people to become more motivated. There is a big difference."

—Tony Spada, President and Chief Executive Officer,
AAA Western and Central New York

"Do you want the answer for how to increase employee engagement at work? You will find it in *CRAVE*. I loved the simple analogies and examples that prove that with the Ultimate Habit process you can make employee recognition and motivation a powerful accelerator of business results. Give them what they CRAVE!"

—Joe Gorman, Division President, East,
Morrison Community Living

"You simply can't get the majority of your employees engaged unless you give them what they CRAVE."

—Kelly Crouse, Vice President of Sales,
The J.M. Smucker Company

"A fantastic read for leaders who are looking to enhance their culture and lead team members to a higher level of performance."

—Scott Bradbary, Chief Talent Officer,
Warren Averett CPA & Advisors

"A fascinating, fast, and easy read. CRAVE provides a great balance of data, business KPIs, and a focus on creating a more positive culture. I loved the science behind what influences more motivation in the workplace."

—Erin Moran, Chief Culture Officer,
Union Square Hospitality Group

CRAVE

You Can Enhance
Employee Motivation in
10 Minutes by Friday™

658.314
L473c

CRAVE

You Can Enhance Employee Motivation in 10 Minutes by Friday™

GREGG LEDERMAN

New York Times, *USA Today*, and *Wall Street Journal*
bestselling author of *ENGAGED!*

Copyright ©2018 by Gregg Lederman

All Rights Reserved.

No part of this book may be reproduced, stored in a retrieval system, or transmitted by any means, electronic, mechanical, photocopying, recording, or otherwise, without written permission from the publisher.

The content of this book has been prepared for informational purposes only. Although anyone may find the ideas, concepts, practices, suggestions, recommendations, disciplines, and understandings presented in this book to be useful, the contents of this book are provided with the understanding that neither the author nor the publisher is engaged in providing any specific business advice to the reader. Nor is anything in this book intended to be a strategy or recommendation for any specific kind of business problem or business opportunity. Each person and business has unique needs, qualities, resources, abilities, and other attributes and this book cannot take these individual differences into account. Each person and business should engage a qualified professional to address their or its unique situation.

CRAVE: You Can Enhance Employee Motivation in 10 Minutes by Friday™

Published by Brand At Work
Cover design by Zoe Maves
Art design by Michael Varouhas
Author photo by Matt Wittmeyer

978-0-9795875-1-1 paperback
978-0-9795875-2-8 ePUB
978-0-9795875-3-5 ePDF

Printed in the United States of America

10 9 8 7 6 5 4 3 2 1

Contents

Acknowledgments xi

What Do We Crave? 1

PART 1: Overwhelming Evidence About What Motivates
Humans at Work 19
   Three Studies as Evidence of What People Crave 20

PART 2: Strategic Employee Recognition: How 10 Minutes
by Friday™ Can Accelerate Business Results 39
   The Recognition Is the Accelerator™ Model 73
   Accelerate Employee Engagement 79
   Accelerate the Work Environment 99
   Accelerate the Customer Experience 135
   Accelerate Business Results 141

PART 3: Mastering the Ultimate Habit™ 147
   Five Steps to Creating A Habit. Simple and Easy! 161
   Step 1: Decide on a Mindset 165
   Step 2: Create Routines and Behaviors 169
   Step 3: Demonstrate Willpower 173
   Step 4: Focus on Benefits 181
   Step 5: Track Effort Daily 185

Appendix 201
Citations 213

Acknowledgments

In writing *CRAVE*, I was fortunate to have access to the wisdom, experiences, and thoughtful perspectives of many individuals. Not only do these people believe in the CRAVE methodology, they advocate for it, striving to perform it in their lives at work as well as at home.

To Courtney Cooley: Once again, you are not just the best but the only person I know who can bring my voice to life while ensuring we stay focused on the key messages and prose readers will most appreciate … all while ensuring the book is well written, grammatically and stylistically. I appreciated your kindness and thoughtfulness as you challenged my assumptions and enhanced this book every step of the way.

To the team at Brand Integrity: Thank you for your continuous passion and commitment to helping our clients fuel their work environments with more of what humans CRAVE: Respect, Purpose, and Relationships. Your expertise in helping to make better workplaces and your willingness to share your experiences working alongside clients provided much of the inspiration and content ideas that are packed into this book.

To our Brand Integrity clients: Without you … this book would have never happened. A great big thank-you to those leaders within our client base who were gracious enough to read the

CRAVE manuscript and provide thoughtful feedback. As well, a heartfelt thank-you to those clients who generously shared their employee, customer, and financial data, allowing me to include real, relevant, and powerful case studies readers will learn from.

To the few dozen pre-readers: I reached out to you because I thought you might have an interesting take on the CRAVE methodology and its applicability in the workplace. And I was humbled and honored that so many of you were motivated to not only read the pre-reader edition, but also to provide volumes of feedback. Your input had a profound impact on this final product.

Last, to my family: Karyn, Caroline, Katie, and Lucy—you are my inspiration! Your joy, energy, and passion for growing as humans and giving to others helped inspire the CRAVE methodology. Your love and support helped me bring it to life in ways others will learn from.

What Do We CRAVE?

The Motivation to Work

For more than eight decades, researchers and scientists have shared what causes humans in the work environment to become more motivated, productive, and focused on the business results their employers want more of. Tons of historical evidence supports similar conclusions (and tons is probably an understatement). What I find fascinating is the gigantic chasm between what science and research prove over and over and what businesses continue to invest in and do (or not do).

In the middle of the last century, three esteemed professors and psychologists, Frederick Herzberg (Western Reserve University), Bernard Mausner (Beaver College), and Barbara Snyderman (University of Pittsburgh School of Medicine) conducted extensive research that should have positively changed the way managers lead in the workforce ... but didn't.

Their research was published in 1959 in the book, appropriately titled, *The Motivation to Work*. Their mission was clear: To discover and help others reinforce the kind of things that make people happier and more productive at work.

They were not alone in this quest, as they cited countless (more than one hundred) previous studies dating back to the 1930s where very smart people uncovered and shared virtually identical findings that were contrary to what business leaders were doing in their attempts to improve workforce motivation.

The Breakthrough That Never Happened

The opening to *The Motivation to Work* states that the findings from their study of job motivation provide breakthrough insights into the nature of job attitudes and behaviors, which profoundly impact employee performance.[1] The authors also share the very specific economic outcomes business leaders should expect from taking action on the learning from their findings. These economic outcomes are very important to consider!

While industry has changed significantly since the mid-1900s, the economic outcomes they highlighted are identical to what businesses chase today (whether stated or not). Herzberg, Mausner, and Snyderman state that one of the goals of their research was to help leaders put into practice work systems to help the workforce "live better and more fruitful lives" while also achieving the following economic benefits:

- more productivity
- decreased employee turnover
- decreased employee absenteeism
- overall better work environment[2]

Sound familiar to you, don't they? Of course they do. They are what leaders at your organization talk about when you are problem solving, strategizing, and planning for the future. Take a look at your existing strategic plans. The key result areas may be coded as "culture improvement," "enhance employee engagement," or "be the employer of choice," but in the end, it's a strategic objective of making an even better place to work in order to drive the business results Herzberg, Mausner, and Snyderman highlighted six decades ago.

One of the challenges preventing their findings from truly being a breakthrough is leaders' inability to learn from or get their teams aligned on the reality of human motivation. They still operate from assumptions about human attitudes, behaviors, and performance that are outdated, unproven, and illogical. They continue to invest (now more than ever—I'll explain shortly) in employee engagement and culture-improving initiatives that are contrary to the mounting evidence that such programs are not only ineffective but, in many cases, do more harm than good with respect to motivating stronger performance. And in most cases, the programs are not focused nearly as much as they should be on driving measurable ROI.

Today, there is no shortage of studies that continue to inform executives about the engagement level of the American workforce. These studies are more advanced technologically than those before them, yet are trying to prove the same hypothesis:

If humans are more motivated at work, they will be more productive and profitable employees.

Regardless of which of the hundreds of studies I could report on from over the past eighty years, the resulting evidence is the same. In fact, the evidence provided in the 1950s was replicated again in the '60s, '70s, '80s, '90s, and 2000s. Decade after decade, researchers and scientists continue to highlight what causes people to be more motivated and committed at work. And decade after decade, businesses continue to struggle to maximize the opportunity these findings present.

> *If humans are more motivated at work, they will be more productive and profitable employees.*

One of the most blogged about and shared studies is Gallup's "State of the American Workforce" (with well over 31 million respondents in its most recent published report). Gallup's findings are nothing short of alarming as they highlight that about two-thirds of the American workforce is not engaged.[3] What makes this even more concerning is that this figure has not changed in the last eighteen years. That's right, in eighteen straight years of measuring employee engagement, the number of engaged employees hasn't budged a noticeable amount.[4]

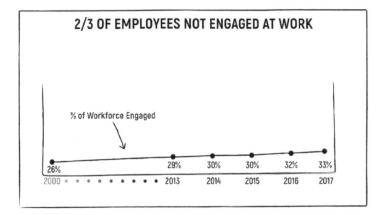

How can this be!? **How can so many Americans still be disengaged at work?**

The answer to the question: **People are not getting nearly enough of what they CRAVE!**

The answer to this question is the heart and soul of this book. The answer, when applied the right way, will positively change your approach to leadership, your work environment, your customer experience, and—most importantly—the business results you want most.

So, what did Herzberg, Mausner, and Snyderman—along with many before them and countless others after them—uncover? They clearly showed that people at work have a few primary motivators that, once fulfilled, lead to more engagement, better

5

work environments, more consistent customer experiences, and better business results.

Here are the top two primary motivators uncovered in their work:

1. **Achievement:** A feeling of accomplishment, making a difference, finding purpose and meaning in one's work; seeing the success of one's work.
2. **Recognition:** When others notice and praise as a showing of respect for doing good work.[5]

These two motivators were far and away more powerful in influencing positive attitudes and motivation in the workplace. Their findings showed that they were respectively 93 percent and 75 percent more impactful than increasing salary in sparking improvements in motivation.[6]

As it turns out, these findings are not at all an anomaly. In fact, these two categories have proved to be top motivators in just about every single study on workforce motivation since ... well ... these studies began in the 1930s. The terminology might change from one study to the next, but in the end, the key factors that drive motivation of humans at work remain the same.

Three Cravings Every Leader Must Know About

My interest in this topic was sparked around ten years ago, and since then I've pored over hundreds of studies, interviewed researchers, and even conducted a few studies of my own to understand what leads to happiness, more motivation, and increased productivity in the workplace. During this time, through my company, Brand Integrity, a leadership development and employee engagement firm, I've worked with thousands of leaders from hundreds of organizations in a quest to increase workplace motivation. In this effort, I've gained a better understanding of what they are doing well and where they are falling short in engaging the hearts and minds of employees.

After studying and digesting eighty-plus years of research and spending nearly two decades working alongside leaders, it became evident that there are three things that humans CRAVE (especially at work)—three things that when employees get them, help them to become happier, more motivated contributors to their organization's success:

1. **Respect:** Help me feel respected for the work I do.
2. **Purpose:** Show me how what I do has purpose, makes a difference, and is relevant to the organization.
3. **Relationship:** Help me build stronger connections with people, especially my immediate manager/supervisor.

As you'll soon see, when humans have these three cravings fulfilled, good things happen: employee engagement, the work culture, and customer experiences all improve. In this book, you will learn how giving people what they CRAVE accelerates the business results you want most. However, doing so is easier said than done.

> *When humans get what they CRAVE,*
> *good things happen.*

The Ultimate Habit™ Helps You Fulfill the Craving

From my experience, leaders who are most successful giving people what they CRAVE are able to master the Ultimate Habit of strategically recognizing employees. The word "strategic" is important and takes on great meaning as part of this habit. By the time you complete this book, you will be in a position to master the Ultimate Habit and do so in as little as 10 Minutes by Friday. That's it! Ten minutes a week or less.

Wait. Before you begin to think about the ways you say thank you to teammates and/or employees or the rewards and recognition programs your organization has invested in, please read on. Together we are going to change the conversation about what employee recognition is, what works, what doesn't, and why you should care. We will go on a journey together where we will prove that the habit of employee recognition is the number one management skill for fueling the work environment with more of what people CRAVE. The type of employee recognition we will explore goes way beyond your typical tchotchkes, pizza parties, and picnics. I'm referring to recognition that is so simple in concept, yet strategic in nature, that it truly becomes a top accelerator of business results.

> *The habit of employee recognition is the number one management skill for fueling the work environment with more of what people CRAVE.*

Herzberg, Mausner, and Snyderman presented what they had hoped would be (and should have been) a breakthrough in understanding and acting on the human condition at work. The breakthrough they proposed never did materialize. A remarkable chasm remains between what scientists and researchers have proved and continue to prove and what businesses continue to do (or not do) when it comes to recognizing employees. As I've said, the information from these studies has been unknown, misunderstood, or simply ignored by leaders for too long. As business leaders, we must stop ignoring the science and start giving people more of what they CRAVE at work. The time is now!

We Love Recognition, But We Are Terrible at It

Whether we want to admit it or not, recognition plays a huge role in our everyday lives: in our happiness and our well-being, both at work and in our personal relationships. Giving and receiving recognition fuels our happiness and our productivity. This makes developing the Ultimate Habit of strategically recognizing employees one of the most effective and affordable ways to provide people what they CRAVE: a greater understanding of the purpose, meaning, and importance of their work and a showing of respect for the effort they provide. When people get more of what they CRAVE, quite simply, they become more motivated and committed. But the problem is, we are terrible at recognition at work. We simply struggle to give it. And most of us don't even know it, which is helping to feed disengagement.

Show of Hands

As a professional speaker, I have the opportunity to be in front of large audiences of managers and leaders of all levels. At almost every speech, I conduct the following experiment and the results are virtually identical every time.

I ask for a show of hands: "How many of you don't like to be recognized when you do a good job?"

Virtually zero hands go up.

Then I ask the audience a follow-up question, again asking for a show of hands: "How many of you are really good at recognizing employees when they do a good job AND ... you do it often enough?"

Having done this experiment more than five hundred times, I would suggest the average hand-raising is somewhere between 5 and 10 percent. Rarely am I able to spark more than 10 percent of leaders' hands to go up.

Maybe you are surprised by this, maybe not. Consider this ... According to recent research:

- 70% of employees say they wish they received more recognition[7]
- 83% of leaders say they could do more to recognize others[8]
- 65% of Americans report they weren't recognized even once last year[9]
- 79% of employees say they would "work harder" if they felt their efforts were better recognized[10]
- 79% of employees who quit their jobs cite a lack of appreciation as a key reason for leaving[11]

Let's Take a Minute to Process the Facts

Am I building the case as to why leveraging the power of recognition as a way to give people what they CRAVE should be your top priority in the immediate future? Yes, I am!

Here's a quick recap about the need to master the habit of recognition:

- For more than eighty years, researchers and scientists keep proving that if people feel recognized, appreciated, and respected for the work they do, and are clearly shown how their work makes a difference, they will be happier and more productive.
- Almost all leaders agree they personally like to be recognized.
- However, most leaders admit they don't do a good job effectively recognizing people at work, at least not often enough.
- The great majority of humans wish they received more recognition at work and say they would work harder if they got it.
- We, as a society, continue to suffer from an employee engagement crisis where motivation levels have not changed in eighteen straight years.

OK... now we are getting somewhere. But we are not there yet. I've already written a book on the engagement crisis. *ENGAGED!* was a *New York Times* best seller a few short years ago. In it, I highlighted an approach for designing a strategic recognition program. It's not your typical, feel-good, tchotchke-driven, rewards-based program. It's a program designed to help managers build relationships and fuel the work environment with what people CRAVE most: genuine appreciation for the work they do, how they do it, and how they make a difference in the world around them.

So far, the Ultimate Habit has helped pay great dividends to many companies. But not nearly enough.

Since 2002, my firm, Brand Integrity, has worked with leaders who want to master the Ultimate Habit of strategically recognizing employees. At the time of this writing, more than 65 percent of our clients are noted as "best places to work" in their industry or region. Keep in mind, during this same span of time researchers have proved over and over that we are in the midst of an engagement crisis with a pathetic 33 percent of workers engaged.[12] However, Brand Integrity clients have experienced a very different engagement outcome. Across all of our clients, the average rate of engagement over the better part of the last decade is 91 percent. I don't share this with you to brag (well, maybe a little). I share this because the power of recognition when done the right way—done strategically—can have significantly positive and sustainable impact.

Not Another Book on Appreciation and Recognition ... Let's Be More Strategic

While there is no shortage of mounting evidence on what people truly CRAVE to become more motivated and committed at work, there is also no shortage of books on the subjects of appreciation and employee recognition. Please trust me ... this book is different.

In *CRAVE*, of course we will cover the "soft" side of recognition, what many refer to as "showing appreciation." But as you've probably experienced, showing appreciation at work can backfire when it's not done genuinely and strategically (key word being "strategically"). In the pages to come, you will learn that when you recognize specific employee actions and link those actions to specific business impacts, you are being strategic. You'll also learn that recognition done wrong will NOT provide what people CRAVE and therefore will not accelerate the results you want most. Unfortunately, as I will get into later on, most organizations are doing recognition programs the wrong way. With that said, the market doesn't need another book on why we should show appreciation at work. There are enough books on this subject. I propose what's needed is a book on how to do recognition the right way: how to make it strategic and how to make it a habit that accelerates business results. And that is what you will find in *CRAVE*!

Are You a Leader, Manager, or Both?

This book says something new. Strategic employee recognition is a management discipline that goes way beyond "being the right thing to do." Recognition should not be viewed only as a feel-good, altruistic endeavor. No, it's a management discipline that should garner significant ROI. Therefore, this book is for leaders. I realize some people have specific definitions they put on the terms leader and manager. Some say a leader sets the vision, focuses on strategy, and inspires others while managers have more responsibility at the task level and focus on day-to-day outcomes. In the past, I have subscribed to the idea that managers get people to do something and leaders get people to become something. However, in this book I will use the terms leader and manager interchangeably. When I refer to a leader or manager, I mean anyone who has earned the right to lead people, process, and/or business outcomes. I am referring to anyone from a frontline supervisory role to an executive in the corner office who is responsible for inspiring humans at work. If you're not yet in a managerial or leadership role, but aspire to be, then you will find the messages and instruction in *CRAVE* will help you advance your career and become the leader you desire to be.

You Have the Power!

If there is one all-encompassing, important message that I hope you take away from this book it's that you as a leader of humans have the power, with very little time investment, to accelerate business outcomes while also positively impacting the lives of people at work. You have the power to give people what they CRAVE by showing them they matter (respect) and what they do matters (purpose), and when you do this you will find it builds stronger relationships. You have the power to help teams, departments, divisions, and an entire organization achieve the results that matter most. But only if you learn to fuel the environment with more of what people CRAVE!

My Promise to You Is This ...

In the prose that follows, I will share how an investment of as little as ten minutes a week can help you masterfully put the Ultimate Habit of strategically recognizing employees to work. That is my promise. When you learn to apply the habit, you will inspire people to do great things. And the personal pride you will feel as a result, when you see others becoming more engaged at work, when you feel the work culture improving, when you witness positive customer reactions ... well, that's when it will hit you. You've mastered a habit that not only accelerates business outcomes but makes you a better leader. Now that is a magical result!

Why the Heck Aren't More People Using the Power of Recognition?

This is a question I've been asking myself for fifteen years. If you've finished reading *CRAVE* and you too are asking this question, then I've done my job. Below are a few reasons I believe leaders are being held back.

First is the true lack of awareness and belief that employee recognition is a management skill to be learned, practiced, and reinforced. All too often it's seen as the soft stuff, and too many leaders think they're good at it when, in reality, they're not.

Second, some leaders act as if an employee must solve world hunger to be recognized and don't see the powerful impact they can have by simply recognizing solid effort as part of a job well done. As you will learn in Part 2, recognition is like a football game: You need a lot of first downs to get touchdowns and lots of touchdowns to win the championship. When it comes to recognizing employees, too many leaders miss the opportunity to recognize those first downs ... those little things people do when they are doing a good job at their job.

Third, like any skill, to optimize the impact, consistency is required, which means a habit is required. And a habit calls for a change of thinking and behaviors. As you may already know, changing behaviors is very hard to do. Think for a moment: What was the most memorable behavior change you've made recently? Let that question simmer. I assure you, we will come back to it.

Three Parts on Your Journey Through CRAVE

The remainder of this book is divided into three parts. In Part 1, I'll touch on the overwhelming evidence from the past eighty years that supports my theory that humans at work have three primary cravings that, once fulfilled, make them happier and enable them to be more motivated and productive at work. The evidence is vast; therefore, I provide a summary overview with a few examples. For those readers who, like me, love the research and want to learn more, I've included an appendix of additional studies for exploring the evolution of behavioral research.

In Part 2, I will guide you through the Recognition Is the Accelerator Model and provide a series of real-life examples of organizations achieving measurable ROI. You will see firsthand the power of strategic recognition to improve employee engagement, the work culture, and the customer experience. In this section, you will also have the opportunity to explore the business results you most want to accelerate. And you will learn how simple it can be with a time investment of as little as ten minutes a week.

Finally, in Part 3, you will learn the steps for mastering the Ultimate Habit of strategically recognizing employees. You will be guided through a step-by-step process with the opportunity to put a plan in place to inspire your success and the success of those around you.

Are you ready? Let's go!

Part 1: Overwhelming Evidence About What Motivates Humans at Work

The More Things Change, the More They Stay the Same

I'm a self-proclaimed research junkie. There is so much to learn from business history and I'm continually intrigued by the reality that the more things change, the more they really do stay the same.

When I began this book, I found myself faced with a mountain of research, starting in the 1930s, that has grown precipitously decade after decade. In this section, I'll share a few examples where you will see how a subset of scholars, not necessarily working in concert yet focused on similar goals, forged new ways of thinking about workplace motivation and what leads to the conditions for humans to generate more of it. I picked these studies because they're in-depth, but simple, and provide compelling evidence of what really drives motivation, productivity, and economic results in the business world. (If you want more, check out the Appendix!)

Quick disclaimer: These studies were conducted in an age during which the workforce was dominated by men. While I can't attest to the number of women who participated, I can say the researchers rarely referenced them while highlighting men as the primary participants. However, I can assure you that as the decades passed, the results remained the same, regardless of gender.

I will highlight two researchers, still active today, who are arguably the most important social scientists of our time. These men are considered pioneers regarding the study of workplace motivation. They introduced a theory in the 1970s, based on three psychological needs, that not only took the existing research to a whole new level but also served as the catalyst for the theory of CRAVE!

THREE STUDIES AS EVIDENCE
OF WHAT PEOPLE CRAVE

1955: People Work to Fulfill a Purpose and Gain a Sense of Accomplishment

In 1955, authors Nancy C. Morse and Robert S. Weiss commissioned a thought-provoking study, "The Function and Meaning of Work and the Job," which highlights all three CRAVE concepts: respect, purpose, and relationship. Morse and Weiss's hypothesis was simple and clear: **"Even if there were no economic necessity for them to work, most men would work anyway."** Their method of data collection included both short surveys and personal interviews. They concluded that 80 percent of workers would continue working, even if they had enough money to be comfortable. But the question remained:

Why? In their words, "The results indicate that for most men working does not simply function as a means of earning a livelihood. Working means having a purpose, gaining a sense of accomplishment and ability to express himself." In their findings, Morse and Weiss summarized three primary reasons men would continue working:

1. Desire to do something interesting
2. Sense of purpose/accomplishment
3. Feeling of self-respect[13]

1957: When Personal Needs Are Satisfied, Employee Turnover Goes Down

Later that same decade, Ian C. Ross and Alvin Zander from the University of Michigan published a study where they set out to prove that there are a few basic needs that, if met, reduce employee turnover and, if not met, lead workers to seek employment elsewhere. Ross and Zander developed a model consisting of five personal needs that people receive from the work environment that most impact employee turnover. And they set out to discover whether people who resign would be less satisfied than those who stay with respect to each of the following needs:

- Recognition
- Affiliation
- Autonomy
- Achievement
- Fair evaluation

They concluded that **"Workers whose personal needs are satisfied on the job are more likely to remain with the organization."**[14]

It is obvious to note that all five personal needs deemed important to job satisfaction, motivation, and staying with the organization are positively connected to the concepts of CRAVE: respect, purpose, and relationship. This connection is easily summarized within a few key points made by Zander and Ross:

- "The need for achievement was interpreted as feeling that one is doing something important when one is working."
- "Those employees who stayed reported having greater acquaintance with management."
- "It is in the area of recognition that we find the largest and most significant difference in degree of satisfaction."[15]

1964: Rewards May Not Work the Way We Think They Do

Here's one more study that is an indication of how little business leaders truly understood about how to drive motivation in the workplace. This was demonstrated by the increased focus on "rewards" as a way to create happier, more motivated and productive employees. In 1964, Daniel Katz published a research study that proved rewards may encourage employees to stay with an organization, but don't necessarily enhance motivation to do better work. If this research was widely read among business leaders (I am confidently assuming it was not), then these leaders would have been left to throw their hands in the air and give up on trying to motivate the workforce. Because there was so little understanding about what really motivates humans, leaders back then (and all too often today) assumed that focusing on pay and other reward-oriented tactics would stimulate stronger performance.

In his work, Katz showed how rewards can have an effect on employee performance that is opposite of what was intended.

> *Rewards do little to motivate performance beyond the line of duty. … The man who finds the type of work he delights in doing is the man who will not worry about the fact that the role requires a given amount of production of a certain quality. His gratifications accrue from accomplishment, from the expression of his abilities, from the exercise of his own decisions.*[16]

Katz highlights several types of what he called "motivational patterns" that increase job satisfaction and play a significant role in influencing motivation and job performance. These include: understanding and following the rules of the game, finding work interesting and gratifying, internalizing organizational goals and values in ways that make them personal, and identifying with a like-minded group.

Who Actually Got to See This Research? Unfortunately, Not Too Many!

The studies I've shared are representative of the many that preceded them and the thousands that followed. These researchers and scientists had very noble causes and uncovered intriguing insights. But how much of this do you think was shared with the people who most needed to learn about it? How many leaders of enterprise do you think ever learned about this research? My guess is … not very many. In fact, from what I can tell, absent the superhighway of information sharing we have today, these researchers probably shared their findings throughout their circles of influence and gave themselves kudos at industry get-togethers. But for the most part they didn't have the chance to see their work successfully applied to have an effect on the general workforce in America. And that is a shame … and still, to some extent, a serious challenge today.

In my opinion, this reality didn't change in the decades that followed. But the amount of research and validating insights continued to grow. Throughout the 1970s, '80s, and '90s, researchers and behavioral scientists continued to prove through field and laboratory studies what influences motivation in the workplace. Yet, the business world didn't widely adopt it. Consider this: Was it that business leaders weren't focused on the right things? Or were they simply acting upon false assumptions about motivation based on lack of information? My guess is the latter.

The Superhighway of Information Is Here. Will That Change Things?

We now have the superhighway of information sharing (the internet), which enables us to share research with one click. Therefore, if my theory is correct, from the 1940s through 2000, the business community was underwhelmed with the facts, while today, we may find ourselves overwhelmed with the amount of research available. For example, I recently read a study mentioned in a blog post that was shared ten thousand times among the business community in two days. Think about that for a moment. If Herzberg, Mausner, and Snyderman wanted to get ten thousand people to read and share *The Motivation to Work* in two days, what kind of effort would that have taken? Can you imagine their delight if they were able to get their self-proclaimed breakthrough research in front of that many business people?

Now let's get to those pioneers I mentioned and the three psychological needs that drive motivation for humans at work.

You May Not Know Them, But Their Work Has Probably Influenced Your Life

I live in Rochester, New York. My company is headquartered here. Rochester is historically a hub of innovation, known for companies such as Kodak (first camera and film), Xerox (the copy machine), and Bausch & Lomb (photographic and optical lenses). Rochester is credited for many other innovations, including the first automobile patent (sorry, Detroit), the automatic voting machine, and—for all you summer camp enthusiasts—boondoggle. Today, Rochester continues to be an innovative community for businesses to flourish with many successful, entrepreneurial companies in the fields of high technology, photonics, optics, and health care.

Rochester also happens to be the home of two innovative social scientists, Edward Deci and Richard Ryan, who are considered the premier thinkers on personal motivation. What did they do to earn this status in their field? Quite simply, they *changed the question* to explore a whole new way of thinking about personal motivation, uncovering three psychological needs all humans have.

Deci and Ryan took the research from the 1950s and 1960s to a whole new level while honoring those before them. In doing so, they've become rock stars in their field. And the crazy thing is… outside of their industry, no one really knows about them.

To further my point: I've been an adjunct professor at the University of Rochester for sixteen years. Deci and Ryan have taught at the school since the 1970s (Deci) and 1980s (Ryan) and their office is a few buildings away from where I teach. Until about seven years ago, I had never heard of them. So, I am going to assume that most people reading this book have also never heard of Edward Deci or Richard Ryan or their motivational theory. However, I can assure you that you've witnessed the effect of their findings in your workplace. And I can promise you, it is their research and the inspiration behind it that helped round out the concept of CRAVE that you will learn about in Part 2 when we cover how to accelerate positive business results.

Allow me to share with you their story, their findings, and how they influenced the study of motivation today.

Rewards Don't Work the Way You Think They Do!

In 1971, after several years of conducting research on the impact of rewards and control tactics on motivation, Edward Deci arrived on the campus at the University of Rochester to take a dual appointment in the psychology department and business school. Deci was on a mission to build upon and prove the theory that external rewards decrease intrinsic motivation. Think about that: Back in 1971, Deci was taking a stand on the idea that using rewards (especially monetary rewards) as a primary way to motivate humans may not work the way people expected them to. And he was determined to prove it. According to Deci, rewards actually thwart the very outcomes you are trying to achieve—that is, get people to tap into their intrinsic motivation and do more of what you want them to do. Deci's initial field studies and experiments were well documented in his 1971 paper,

"The Effects of Externally Mediated Rewards on Intrinsic Motivation." This paper kicked off his career, which as of this writing has culminated in eleven books and hundreds of research papers either authored by him or featuring his work.

In 1973, the business school at the university called "heresy" on Deci's work and abruptly removed him from his research and teaching duties. Apparently, they could not wrap their heads around the idea that rewarding performance was not the primary driver of motivation. Fortunately, the psychology department was interested in hiring him full time. In the years that followed, Deci gained momentum in his work, publishing his first book on the subject, simply and appropriately titled *Intrinsic Motivation*.

The study of motivation really took off in 1977 when Richard Ryan, then a student in the clinical psychology department at the University of Rochester, connected with Deci who at the time was teaching a class on Gestalt therapy. Together, they began running workshops on the subject. Ryan explained:

> *I had a philosophical interest in the impact of autonomy on personal motivation and shared that with Ed, knowing he'd been doing research on the subject. Then one day I came across a used book titled* Intrinsic Motivation, *began reading it, and became even more intrigued. At the time, I didn't realize Ed had written it. Once I did realize*

that, I invited him to lunch and said, "You didn't tell me you wrote a book on the subject." And he replied, "You never asked."

From there, a very special relationship took off, leading to a more than forty-year research partnership focused on proving that, contrary to traditional thinking, monetary rewards are not usually the primary driver of motivation and in fact can sometimes undermine humans' intrinsic motivation. By 1981, the two began publishing their first studies together. Richard Ryan also joined forces with the faculty at the University of Rochester, where he is still a research professor in the psychology department today.

Together, this dynamic duo created the framework that has changed the way millions of people think about motivation in the workplace (as well as many other aspects of life). They coined it Self-Determination Theory.

Self-Determination Theory is focused on the social and work environment conditions that lead humans to tap into more of their personal motivation. There's nothing sexy about the research or the way Deci and Ryan packaged up their findings. They purposefully didn't put a lot of flash and pizzazz or aggressive marketing around it. However, the applicability of what they uncovered provides tremendous opportunity to influence the way people manage and lead others—especially in the work environment.

Deci and Ryan conducted or influenced many studies revealing that people do not perform as well at problem solving when they are working for an external reward than they do when they are intrinsically motivated. In fact, several studies confirmed that performance of any activity that requires resourcefulness, deep concentration, intuition, or creativity is likely to be impaired when controls are used as a motivational strategy. They were also quick to point out the importance of understanding that rewards and other controls do have motivating power, but with limitations. People's behavior can, at least to some extent, be controlled in the sense that people will do what they have to in order to get a reward, avoid punishment, or win a competition.

With that said, we must be mindful of the reality that there are problems with relying on rewards and controls to motivate people. Most notable: Once you decide to use rewards to control people, you can't easily go back. The research shows the behavior will last only as long as the rewards are forthcoming. But in most cases at work, the activities we reward are ones that we would like to keep going long after the rewards have stopped. The second problem is that once people are oriented toward rewards, they will all too likely take the shortest or quickest path to get them. Usually, however, the shortest path is not what we hope to promote.

Deci and Ryan highlight two types of motivation they refer to as controlled and autonomous. Controlled motivation is basically the carrot and stick. With controlled motivation, you've likely been seduced or coerced into doing something. When controlled motivation is used in the workplace, employees tend to feel a sense of pressure and anxiety that comes with negative consequences to performance and well-being. In contrast, there is autonomous motivation. When employees experience a sense of choice about what they are doing—if they are endorsing their own behavior—then they are likely to find more interest and enjoyment in that activity. This increases willingness to provide the effort. Another type of autonomous motivation highlighted in Deci and Ryan's research has to do with deeply held values and beliefs. If an employee has beliefs that align with the activity they are tasked with doing, then tapping into their intrinsic motivation in ways that support those beliefs is considerably easier to do.

Deci and Ryan are quick to point out that there are literally hundreds and hundreds and hundreds of scientific investigations that support their findings that when a human is autonomously motivated, their behavior will be more creative, they will be a better problem solver, and they will perform better. In addition, autonomous motivation lends itself to more positive emotions and is associated with improvements in both physical and psychological health and well-being.

But Back to Money for a Moment

Quick disclaimer about money: Money is important and mission critical to the employee workplace contractual relationship. People are not going to work for free simply because you are giving them what they CRAVE. However, here is the reality to keep in mind as you learn about Self-Determination Theory. You must pay people at least the market wage for their position/role in the company. And, by the way, today people can go online and figure out within minutes the going wage for their role within their industry and geographic region. Therefore, as you learn about the work of Deci and Ryan, understand that once an employee knows they are paid a fair market wage, the real issue driving motivation is whether they feel some basic human needs are being met.

Let's dive into Self-Determination Theory, what it is, and why it matters. To begin, let's explore the question Deci and Ryan asked that sparked a change in thinking about human motivation.

Change the Question ... Uncover What Really Motivates Humans

Arguably the most important thing that Deci and Ryan did early on in their partnership was change the question researchers were asking for decades. Instead of asking, *how can people motivate others?* (which implies that motivation is something that is done to people), they asked a new question built upon the idea that motivation is something inside of humans and that conditions (the environment) are what encourage people to tap into it. With this in mind, Deci and Ryan made a subtle, yet significant change by asking: ***How can people create the conditions where others will motivate themselves?*** This was a subtle, yet significant, change that would enable their future studies (and the studies of many others) and ultimately position them as true pioneers in the study of motivation.

With the new question framework in mind, Ryan and Deci continued their journey to uncover what those conditions would be to help humans tap into more of their personal motivation. Their studies in various settings determined that when constructive feedback and communication are provided, they induce feelings of competence that enhance intrinsic motivation. On the other hand, when negative performance feedback is given, it diminishes motivation. Through these experiments and studies, they refined their theory to define the simple, straightforward psychological needs humans require to maximize motivation— needs that have nothing at all to do with motivation by fear, control tactics, or money. This was the birth of the theory that I (and thousands of others) am building off of today.

The Birth of a Theory

Self-Determination Theory is grounded in the human condition based on the notion of universal human needs. It argues that we have three innate psychological needs: competency, autonomy, and relatedness. If we want to become more self-motivated, self-directed, happier, and more productive, then we need to find ways to satisfy those needs in ourselves and in others. In contrast, when we don't feel these basic, psychological needs are met—or worse, when they are thwarted in some way (which happens a lot at work)—then our happiness, motivation, and commitment will suffer.

Below is a short summary of each of the psychological needs that Self-Determination Theory comprises:

1. **Competence:** A feeling of accomplishment when a challenging task is taken on and performed successfully.
2. **Autonomy:** A feeling of choice that engenders willingness. It encourages people to fully endorse what they are doing.
3. **Relatedness:** A feeling of importance, pertinence, significance, and relevancy.

According to Deci and Ryan:

> *Our findings are of great significance for individuals who wish to facilitate the motivation of others in a way that engenders commitment, effort, and high-quality performance. Furthermore, we've shown that employees' experience of satisfaction of the needs of autonomy, competence and relatedness in the workplace predicted stronger performance and well-being at work.*[17]

For the purposes of this book, I'm focused on Self-Determination Theory and how it applies in the business realm. I would be remiss if I didn't point out that the business world is not the only focus for Deci, Ryan, and many other practitioners conducting studies and publishing research in support of this topic. With a simple Google search or by visiting www.selfdeterminationtheory.org, you can find practitioners in the fields of education, psychotherapy, psychopathology, sports and exercise, gaming, and health and well-being, among others.

Even with all of these fields of study, it pains me to say that Deci and Ryan's work remains largely unknown in the field of business. This is a shame because their findings clearly show that motivation produces results in the work environment and therefore should be of preeminent concern to those responsible for managing and leading humans.

To Create the Work Environment for Motivation, Give People What They CRAVE

As you've read, the basic premise of Deci and Ryan's work is that if more efforts are focused on creating the environment where humans' basic needs are met, motivation will increase. This is why I've embraced their work as the foundation of the theory of CRAVE. When it comes to creating the work environment for more motivation and commitment from the workforce, CRAVE is inclusive of all three of the basic psychological needs that Deci, Ryan, and their arsenal of disciples have proved in the past and continue to prove in their research today. When you consider each component of Self-Determination Theory (autonomy, competence, relatedness), you'll see there is a connection to each of the three CRAVE concepts. I shared this perspective in a recent conversation with Richard Ryan. We talked about how analogous our theories were and walked through how each of the basic psychological needs identified in Self-Determination Theory fulfills the cravings humans have for respect, purpose, and relationship.

Autonomy Fulfills the CRAVING

As a leader, you can't provide autonomy without respecting the work of the employee. The employee must have some sense of purpose behind the work they do if they are to generate the necessary willingness to get excited about their role and perform at a consistently high level. When you as a manager allow self-direction, you are showing the employee you trust them, which in most cases can't help but improve the trust they have in you, enhancing the relationship on both sides.

Competence Fulfills the CRAVING

When leaders help employees realize the success of their efforts, they spark feelings of accomplishment and confidence, which helps the employee feel respected for the work they are doing and how they got it done. In addition, if the work is important (and hopefully it is, or the job would not be a priority for the organization), they gain the sense of purpose that comes from knowing they matter and making the connection between what they do and the success of their team, department, or organization. And of course, when leaders help create a feeling of accomplishment, this also paves the road to more trusting relationships.

Relatedness Fulfills the CRAVING

Deci and Ryan define relatedness as a feeling of importance, pertinence, significance, and relevancy. When people feel cared about, when they care for others, or when they have a sense of belonging to a group that is important to them, they garner a sense of relatedness. If an employee's work is important, a sense of belonging and purpose is easier to come by. When one feels their work has significance, they more likely feel they are doing work others care about and therefore feel respected for that work. And last, to feel a sense of belonging at work assumes strong relationships.

After taking Richard Ryan through my thesis he looked right at me and said, "I think it's a perfect fit." I agreed!

I've only touched the surface of Deci and Ryan's half century of work. My goal was to introduce you to their theory and show how it helped drive the concept of CRAVE. But there is much more to their story. Deci and Ryan gave me personal interviews to tell me about their work and the hundreds of disciples who continue to create communities focused on uncovering and applying the key drivers of motivation in a variety of walks of life. You can find this in the Appendix. Don't skip it just because you've completed *CRAVE*. It's super interesting!

Part 2: Strategic Employee Recognition: How 10 Minutes by Friday™ Can Accelerate Business Results

If you want to see more of something, recognize the actions that lead to it.

Change the Conversation to Convert Doubters to Believers

Two years ago, I sat in the office with Matt, the CEO of a health care organization. He started our meeting saying:

> *I understand recognizing employees is important. It makes employees feel good and if they feel good they might perform better. I see our recognition efforts as a necessary expense today. However, sometimes I think our employees expect too much and I'm worried we spend too much.*

It was now time for me to "change the conversation" with Matt. By the end of our meeting, Matt would go from thinking of employee recognition as an expense to understanding how strategically recognizing employees is a primary accelerator for the business results he wants to achieve.

Matt was a Recognition Results Doubter. He didn't doubt that it was a nice thing to do. He simply doubted the positive financial impact it could have if performed the right way. My job was to convert Matt from a doubter to a believer.

Are You a Secret Recognition Results Doubter?

Do you work with a Recognition Results Doubter? Are you secretly a doubter? If so, don't worry. I am on a mission with the goal of getting every reader to ask, "Why the heck aren't more people using the power of recognition?" You'll get there!

Being a doubter has nothing to do with intelligence.

Intellectually, most people get it pretty quickly. If you recognize employees for good work, you will see more of that good work. When people are appreciated, they feel better about themselves and it should translate into better performance. But there is a lot more to it.

In order to get the conversation on the right track—one that would end with a sharp focus on business results—I shared this perspective with Matt: "If you want to see more of something, recognize the actions that lead to it." Then I asked, "What is your 'something'? What results do you want to see improved?"

Matt quickly rattled off the results his organization wanted. They were the kind of results typical for any health care organization to strive to achieve:

- Less staff turnover and absenteeism (especially among nurses)
- Better patient experience scores
- Improved quality scores

Matt paused and said, "We need more employees who work hard and truly understand what it means to 'do a great job.'"

Now that I had Matt's "something" out on the table, it was time to hit him with the evidence. That is, the eight-plus decades of research covered in Part 1. The years of data that prove over and over again that if you want to create a more engaged work-force—with employees who are motivated and committed to your success, to your customers, and to the goals of your organization—then you must give them what they CRAVE!

I shared with Matt two of the things humans CRAVE at work (respect and purpose) and explained how when employees get them, they become more loyal, more motivated, and more committed.

Then I asked, "What area of your workforce could most benefit from a boost in respect and a better understanding of the purpose and importance of their work? What area, where if they received more of what they CRAVE, might lead to less turnover, better patient scores, and overall improved quality?"

Matt said, "We sure would like to see less turnover among the nurses we hire. We hire very talented people, we invest heavily in training them, and then all too often they leave within the first six months. It's a very difficult job, but to leave within six months is costly to our organization."

Matt's right; it sure is expensive to retain a nurse. The average cost to replace a registered nurse (RN), which includes recruiting, hiring, and training, ranges from $38,900 to $59,700, and it is estimated that health care institutions are losing between $5 million and $8 million annually. This reality gives Matt (and any leader in health care) great reason to be concerned. The two primary nursing positions, RN and CNA (Certified Nursing Assistant), suffer from high annual turnover at 14.6 percent and 24.6 percent respectively.[18]

Given these very high costs and the opportunity to make positive change happen, Matt and his leadership team committed to learning and applying the Ultimate Habit to recognize nurses more often. For a few years, they had tried to implement an online, social recognition platform, but found most managers and leaders didn't use it. So, a renewed commitment was made. The goal was ten minutes a week to stop, think about a success that a nurse was involved in, and acknowledge and share the success with others.

Our work teams quickly highlighted the types of actions managers should watch out for as opportunities for recognition. These actions ranged from contributing to good customer (patient) service, improving quality of care, helping out other teammates, improving processes, and following existing processes in a way that made for a better work experience.

Over the next two years, leaders stepped up their efforts, paying special attention to seeing and sharing successes of those in the nursing role. Leaders increased the number of recognitions for nurses in their online social platform by 133 percent. This added effort averaged out to a few minutes a week for a committed manager. That's it … only a few minutes a week.

The results were astonishing: A 29 percent decrease in nurse turnover. A 13 percent increase in customer loyalty scores. Quality scores steadily improved as well. And while nurses were a primary focus, Matt and his team found recognition activity increased throughout the entire organization as 94 percent of managers leveraged the power of using strategic recognition to give people more of what they CRAVE. This led to more than 75 percent of the workforce joining in the effort to recognize others and be recognized. The result? Turnover began to drop in other areas—in some cases by as much as 50 percent!

133% increase in strategic recognition accelerates 29% drop in employee turnover

I met with Matt about the results they achieved over the two-year period. He was no longer a Recognition Results Doubter ... he was a full believer. "It's clear," he said. "Recognition done well goes far beyond a feel-good endeavor."

By taking the time to spot nurses (and other employees) living their core values, demonstrating the skills and service standards that make for a better place to work and better customer experience, Matt and his team were able to show respect for employees' work, as well as help them better see and understand the purpose and importance of that work.

Recognize what you want to see more of.

What If I Could Offer You a Genie?

But as with most genies, there's a catch … you can wish for only one of two things:

1. *A 50 percent improvement in the business outcome of your choice over the next twelve months.* You can choose any improvement in your business: revenue, EBITDA, overall profitability, customer satisfaction or loyalty scores, employee engagement, quality, safety, machine uptime, fewer costly mistakes, etc.

2. *The ability to replicate your best employees.* With this wish, you can replicate the way your best employees think, speak, and act.

Which would you choose?

I've been posing this question to audiences of leaders for more than ten years. At first thought, I am sure some people consider the first wish. A 50 percent increase in a business result over twelve months does sound quite enticing. For some, they could look like a real hero at work. But what happens after the twelve months? With the second wish, you have the ability to replicate the way your best people think, speak, and act, increasing the number of people doing things the way you want them done, helping you achieve the results most important to your success. (Clearly the second wish is the better one, unless of course you are retiring in the coming year or are already planning to look for another job.)

The reality is, you don't need a genie—you can replicate your best people with the power of strategic recognition.

Stop Rationing Out Praise

Think for a moment about how natural it is to recognize achievements in small children. Consider a one-year-old child. Let's call him Johnny. When Johnny is one and takes his first steps, what do we do? We praise him like crazy. When little Johnny finally gets on that bike and takes off on his own, what do we do? We praise him like crazy. When Johnny brings home his first report card packed with good grades, what do we do? We praise him like crazy. Why? Because he was successful and if we want to see more success, we must recognize it when we see it.

I am sharing examples that occur many years apart. But we all know we feel like a better parent when we recognize kids regularly for their achievements.

Throughout life, this pattern continues. Next Johnny gets involved in extracurricular activities. Maybe he learns an instrument, plays a sport, or joins the theater group. He has more success and what do we do? We provide him the recognition he CRAVES and deserves. And this helps him to become a better human. A more productive member of society. Maybe Johnny goes off to college and if he does, the pattern continues even further. He gets regular recognition for his efforts and results.

He gets what he CRAVES. Then, after college, Johnny gets his first job. That's when something interesting begins to happen.

Now Johnny enters the workforce where the phrases "good job" and "way to go" are simply not used enough. All too often leaders falsely think they don't have the time and/or are Recognition Results Doubters. Either way, they end up rationing out praise as if there will be a shortage of it when they could be using strategic recognition to replicate their best people.

Stop rationing out praise as if there will be a shortage of it when you could be replicating your best people.

Millennials Are Screaming for More Respect and Purpose

Between 1981 and 1996, approximately 73 million millennials were born.[19] [20] Also known as Generation Y and sometimes called Gen Next, they are critical to accelerating business results as they already make up one-third of the workforce and that number is expected to grow to 75 percent by 2025.[21] [22] Business leaders across the globe are talking a lot about this generation, trying to understand their attitudes and beliefs and to make sense of their behaviors. They want to apply this knowledge to create more employee engagement, better customer experiences, and of course … better business results.

And while millennials certainly differ in some ways—from an attitude and behavior standpoint—they largely want the same things as Boomers and Generation X. They are looking for growth opportunities, good managers who care about them, and jobs that are well-suited to their talents and interests. And as you'll see in the pages that follow, when we really dissect what's most important to this group, we will find their cravings remain the same as that of their older counterparts: **Show me respect and help me see the purpose and meaning of my work.**

The big difference might be that millennials want even more of it and show up at work each day with expectations that they should receive it. This presents an opportunity for forward-thinking and savvy leaders who take the steps to learn what millennials care about and adopt work systems that help create the environment where they get it. Why fight it? You are that forward-thinking leader (and maybe you are a millennial too) and it's your job to create the environment for employees to thrive. Knowing some of the basics of what millennials want (and expect) is important to your success as a leader.

What Do Millennials Want?

The evidence is clear. Millennials don't just work for a paycheck—they want purpose and meaning in their work. I'm not suggesting that other generations don't—as a matter of fact, they do. Millennials, however, are a bit more insistent. This idea that they want the same things older generations want, just a little more, is a recurring theme in the research on this group.

Like generations before them, millennials want a great life and jobs they enjoy. They care a lot about relationships and desire to work with people they like, especially managers. And they want to be engaged at work—emotionally and behaviorally. But an important question we must ask is, are they engaged at work?

Recognize Me! That's What I Want Most. And You Should Too!

Millennials are the least engaged generation in the workforce, with only 29 percent being emotionally connected to their jobs and organization and 55 percent categorized as "not engaged." Worse, an additional 16 percent of millennials are actively disengaged, meaning their attitude, lack of care, and/or behaviors may actually do damage to their organization.[23]

Not unexpectedly, this lack of engagement keeps millennials on a constant lookout for "what's next." Research says 60 percent of millennials are open to different job opportunities, which is 15 percentage points higher than non-millennial workers. "Many millennials likely don't want to switch jobs, but their companies are not giving them compelling reasons to stay. When they see what appears to be a better opportunity, they have every incentive to take it."[24]

The Ultimate Habit of strategically recognizing employees is important to perform with all generations. Everyone wants more recognition. A study conducted with over 1,000 employees across the U.S. asked, "What is the most important thing your manager or company does (or could do) that would cause you to produce Great Work?" Responses were bucketed into common themes. The number one response was "recognize me," which was cited 37 percent of the time—nearly three times more often than any other response in the survey and more than five times more than the responses that fell into the theme of "pay me more." Not surprising that "recognize me" was also the most popular response for millennials, also at about three times the frequency of the next highest response theme.[25] [26]

> *Recognition is the most important thing a manager can do to encourage millennial workers.*

Not a Surprise ... Millennials Want Purpose, Communication, and Technology

Here is a simple way to bucket the top three notable differences with millennials that should be taken into consideration when demonstrating the Ultimate Habit to give them what they CRAVE.

First, millennials are direct in their desire to work for companies that are purposeful in the way they operate and in the products and services they deliver. According to one study, 60 percent cite "a sense of purpose" as a reason for choosing their current employer.[27]

Second, millennials want frequent communication. And leaders should want to provide it. Why? Because it has been proven that more frequent communication, especially in the form of recognition and praise, leads to higher performance for individuals, teams, and organizations. According to Gallup: "Forty-four percent of millennials who report that their manager holds regular meetings with them are engaged, while only 20% of millennials who do not meet regularly with their manager are engaged."[28]

So, if you can get more than twice the engagement level from millennials by simply meeting with them a little more often and strategically recognizing their success, then why in the world wouldn't you? Bottom line, the more conversations managers have with their millennial employees, the more engaged they become. And strategically recognizing employees provides a terrific forum to spark meaningful conversations.

Third, technology provides a notable difference among generations. Not just any technology, but the day-to-day technology that sparks collaboration and connection.

We Are All Technology Addicts. The New Norm at Work

Millennials are first-generation digital natives who feel completely at home on the internet and with the use of technology in the workplace. It's all they've known throughout their educational and work lives. Eighty-seven percent of this generation access the internet from their smartphones—considerably more than any other generation.[29]

This generation is accused of being technology addicts and I believe they are. But, from my experience, so is my generation (Gen X). Even so ... millennials seem to be even more addicted. A recent study revealed that 91 percent of millennials believe they have a healthy relationship with their technology. However, 79 percent also say they sleep with their phones and more than half (53 percent) say they wake up at least once per night to check their phones.[30] Now, I don't want to be judgmental ... OK, maybe a little ... but I can't get comfortable with the idea that sleeping with a phone and getting up at least once a night to check it is helpful in providing the mind and body the optimal rest for high performance at work. Regardless of what I think, this is the most wired generation, and the generations that follow are going to be even more wired. So, we need to adopt work systems and technology that help maximize engagement and productivity in the workplace.

According to a PwC report, "Millennials expect the technologies that empower their personal lives to also drive communication and innovation in the workplace." Not surprising, then, that 41 percent would rather communicate with others electronically when compared to face-to-face or talking on the phone. And 78 percent say using technology at work makes them more effective.[31] This means that millennials in the workplace expect to use the same platforms that they are used to (social networks, instant messaging, blogs, etc.). And the nice thing is, each of these technologies, when used appropriately, can help leaders create the environment where more millennials (and older generations and future generations) get what they CRAVE.

To recap, millennials have the same cravings as all employees in the workplace. The same cravings that Herzberg, Mausner, Snyderman, Morse, Ross, Weiss, Zander, Katz, Deci, Ryan, and countless others have proved are innate, human needs that support greater motivation to perform. However, my thesis is that there are a few key strategies for giving millennials *a little bit more*. Keep these in mind as you embark on the journey of creating the Ultimate Habit of strategically recognizing employees:

1. Connect them to the purpose and meaning of their work.
2. Communicate frequently.
3. Provide technology that fosters collaboration.

Wait.

Before we move on, let's cover a few predictions about the next generation that will proliferate our workforce: Generation Z!

Gen Z: Similar to Millennials. But Maybe a Little Different

In the years ahead, an unprecedented four distinct generations will be working together at the same time: baby boomers, Gen X, millennials, and Gen Z. The research on Gen Z, our newest cohort of humans joining the workforce, is picking up steam. Plenty of initial studies are conducted every day throwing out data points, insights, and speculations that make their way into articles and spread quickly across the blogosphere.

At the time of this writing, many things are still unclear. For one, our society has not yet made a clear distinction on the time frame for this generation. Some say it's those born between 1990 and 1999, while others suggest 1995 to 2010 is more appropriate. You'll even find some generational prognosticators pushing the timeline even further to 1998 to 2016. For our purposes, and to stay in alignment with what's been decided on millennials (1981 to 1996), I'm going with the time frame of the mid-1990s through the early 2000s where an unbelievable 72.8 million individuals are beginning to enter the workforce.[32] That's right, just when we thought we figured out millennials, Generation Z is here, and they are moving in fast and furious.

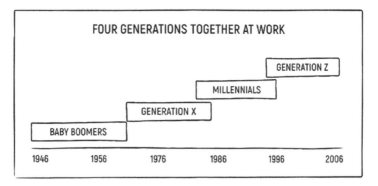

Disclaimer: My wife Karyn and I are raising three Gen Zers born in 2000, 2002, and 2006. I've watched our three wonderful daughters grow through the years, paying particular attention to how they interact with family, friends, teammates, and new acquaintances. So naturally I come to this portion of the book with some bias that influences any predictions made on the future reality and impact of this workforce. Based on research reviewed and my own experience, it's obvious that Gen Z has a lot in common with millennials, but there are also a few ways in which these generations may be uniquely different.

Predictions: This Is What Generation Z Will Want from the Workplace

Similar to millennials, Gen X, and boomers, Gen Z will want and expect growth opportunities, good managers who care about them, and jobs that are well-suited to their talents and interests. In addition, what's been highlighted over the years that seems to matter most and differentiate millennials will also be of utmost importance: meaningful work, frequent communication, and technology that fosters collaboration.

Below are four predictions of what to expect when welcoming the newest group of budding entrepreneurs and corporate climbers into the workplace:

1. **Want safety and stability:** These young people grew up through the Great Recession, which means they may have witnessed the stress, worry, and financial setback their parents faced. They may end up being even more motivated by job security and money.

2. **Desire independence:** Some researchers are speculating these young folks prefer to have office space to themselves, rather than an open, collaborative workspace. This surprised me at first. But then I began to think about how much time kids today spend "being social" while alone, as they communicate via a variety of social sites that bring individuals and groups together. In my opinion, this is the most fascinating prediction to watch.

3. **Expect to have to work hard:** While millennials are known for collaboration, we may find this generation may be less focused on teamwork. They are accustomed to working on their own and even desire doing so. We may find they want to be judged on their own merits, rather than those of their team. According to a study by Enactus, an international nonprofit organization dedicated to inspiring

students to improve the world, 77 percent of Gen Z feel they will need to work harder than previous generations.[33] All generations are told they need to work hard. But this one might hear it *a little bit more*.

4. **Prefer face-to-face communications:** This is the prediction I am least confident in, but think is worthy of making as it could have a big impact on communication tactics in the workplace. The Enactus study also found that the majority of Gen Z employees say they prefer in-person discussions over instant messaging or email.[34] This surprised me given this generation's obvious desire and ability to multitask through the day in an über-connected world (the only world they've ever lived in). They are accustomed to receiving constant updates from dozens of apps, and switching among a variety of tasks is the norm. Paying simultaneous attention to a wide range of stimuli comes more naturally to them. Just yesterday I walked into my oldest daughter's room and she was texting, watching Netflix, and preparing for a psychology test all at one time. This used to surprise me. But I've seen this talent before. I'm no longer surprised. Maybe a bit alarmed. But not surprised. Let's wait and see if this prediction of face-to-face communication as a preference comes true.

The next decade will prove to be an interesting one as the four generations begin to coexist together at work. For the purpose of this book, it's important to keep a few things in mind. First, these generations are still more alike than unalike with respect to what they CRAVE. You'll find zero research on any workforce group that would suggest humans don't want leaders to show them respect, help them see how their work has purpose and meaning, or do not desire strong, healthy relationships, especially with direct supervisors and managers.

Second, it doesn't matter what generation you're in: The science shows that we all benefit from being recognized in ways that fulfill that unanimously desired craving.

What the Science Tells Us

Until now, I've shared the social science behind human psychological needs that, when fulfilled, enhance motivation. There's more to it than this. From a biological perspective, the science tells us the same thing.

Dopamine, serotonin, and oxytocin are a threesome of brain chemicals that influence our feelings. Not at all surprisingly, they are released when we feel respected for the work we do, understand the purpose and relevance of that work, and build strong relationships with those we work with. This threesome directly impacts our motivation and productivity. And while many events can trigger these neurotransmitters, strategically recognizing employees can put you in the driver's seat to creating more motivation in the workplace.

I'm not going to try to get super scientific with you. However, a plethora of research exists on what triggers the release of each of these neurochemicals. For our purposes, let's summarize the key concepts.

According to Dr. Loretta Graziano Breuning, professor emerita of management at California State University, our happiness comes from "happy chemicals" triggered in our brain when we see something good for our survival. Dr. Breuning, in her book *Habits of a Happy Brain*, points out that each chemical comes with a different good feeling:

1. Dopamine produces the joy of finding things that meet your needs—the "Eureka! I got it!" feeling.
2. Serotonin produces the feeling of being respected by others—a feeling of pride.
3. Oxytocin produces the feeling of being safe with others—often described as bonding.
4. Endorphins produce oblivion that masks pain—often called euphoria.[35]

As we tackle the power you have to unleash increases in brain chemicals that have an impact on both your life and the lives of those around you, I will cover the first three "happy chemicals." The fourth (endorphins) is not as heavily influenced by recognition in the work environment. Let's look and see how the interplay of these brain chemicals can help you get and give more of what we all CRAVE!

Dopamine Increases Happiness and Motivation

Dopamine is one of the chemicals regulating the pleasure center of the brain. It is a major force contributing to our motivation as it sends signals to receptors in the brain saying, "This feels good!" This chemical is released anytime we hear, feel, or see something we like. Its primary function is to make us pursue happiness. This is quite different from "make us happy." When you walk into the kitchen and smell fresh-baked cookies, what do you begin to crave? Cookies. You may not even be hungry, but the release of dopamine kick-starts that craving. When you receive a text message or check your Facebook to see how many "likes" you received, a small shot of dopamine is released. When you're feeling down, what do you do to feel better? If you're like most people, you turn to the promise of reward— dopamine releasers like eating, drinking alcohol, shopping, watching TV, playing video games, surfing the internet, etc. All activities that promise to make us feel better. Until they don't. When we overindulge in any of these activities, we experience unintended consequences in the form of a dopamine hangover, which represents itself as guilt or a longing for true happiness.

Dopamine is highly addictive as the behaviors it reinforces can actually do us harm. Most notable are the struggles people face with respect to addictive drugs, nicotine, alcohol, and gambling. Partaking in these behaviors releases dopamine—and lots of it. That's why the feeling we get can be intoxicating and very hard to break from.

But releasing dopamine isn't associated only with negative activities, and you can naturally release it in positive and healthy ways. For example, certain foods result in dopamine boosts as do things like exercising, meditating, listening to music, petting a dog, or working on a hobby.

In the work environment, recognition for a job well done provides a healthy small increase in dopamine, enabling people to get what they CRAVE.

Dopamine motivates us to take action toward personal and business goals as we get a rush of pleasure when we achieve them. This powerful chemical is responsible for the feeling of satisfaction after we've given a solid effort or completed a project knowing we've done good work. The feeling of making progress or being successful is primarily because of dopamine.

As a leader, when you take the few moments to spot a successful achievement, whether it's a little extra effort or an accomplishment (small or large), and you acknowledge and share your opinion, you enable that dopamine rush for the employee. They receive your recognition of their effort and their brain rewards them with a hit, which encourages them to keep going and work even harder to be successful in hopes of more dopamine later on. Dopamine (the brain's hope for more of it) encourages more of the ideal behaviors necessary to achieving the business results you and the team care about.

You are spiking a dopamine release when you say, "Hey Emily, nice job double-checking that paperwork before it went to the shop floor. Your efforts help us to live our core value of being Operationally Excellent, and also help us keep those machines running at full capacity while decreasing the chances of quality mishaps. You are doing a great job. Keep it up!" What Emily thinks is "Fantastic! They respect me for the work I do, and I make a difference to our organization's success." That, of course, is the dopamine talking.

As a leader, when you share a success, recognizing the accomplishments of your team or individuals on it, you are providing a dopamine reward that increases their happiness and future motivation.

As a leader, you can enable a dopamine rush for employees with recognition.

A Serotonin Boost Sparks Pride

The chemical responsible for our moods is serotonin. Not having enough of it has been proven to lead to depression and anxiety. Serotonin levels are heavily influenced when we feel valued and appreciated.

Mood-altering drugs such as ecstasy and LSD cause massive rises in serotonin levels, which of course can be quite unhealthy. However, there are many positive ways to get small increases in serotonin, which also fulfills our craving for being respected and understanding the purpose and meaning of our work.

When serotonin is absent or when the brain doesn't release enough of it, we often experience loneliness and depression. Researchers have shown that increases in serotonin are tied to when people feel significant, important, and/or a sense of pride. Consider this... the feeling of pride at work is a feeling we get when we perceive that others like or respect us. This feeling makes us feel strong and confident.

In her work, Dr. Breuning concluded, "Getting respect feels good because it triggers serotonin."[36] She encourages us to stimulate our own serotonin boosts by taking a few moments each day to express pride in something we've accomplished. Breuning suggests:

> *Stop once a day to appreciate your good effect on others. Don't call attention to it or say, "I told you so." Simply look for your subtle influence and feel satisfied. If you do this for forty-five days, you will feel satisfied by your ability to influence the world and you will feel less frustrated by other people's flaws and neglect. You will have a mental pathway to feel good about your social importance.*[37]

As it turns out, this advice is quite common among scientists and researchers who regularly suggest focusing on past achievements and victories as a way to boost serotonin levels. The fact is, we all want to feel valued for the effort we put forth and for the results we achieve.

The sad reality is that we shouldn't have to exclusively rely on ourselves as Dr. Breuning suggests.

This is where you come in as the leader with the power to provide a little "mood-altering" gratitude that boosts serotonin. Consider it your job as a leader to spot moments where employees should feel good about the work they are doing and make it a point to tell them (and others) about it.

A Hit of Oxytocin Creates Connectedness

Known as the "trust" chemical that helps create healthy relationships, oxytocin is activated by positive social interactions. In the work environment, it helps motivate us to work together to achieve common goals.

Acts of kindness also encourage the production of oxytocin. This means that when you invest the time as a leader to recognize the success of others, you get a hit of oxytocin as well. What a wonderful, win-win situation. You get to provide people what they CRAVE and, in return, you get a little shot of "feel-good" as well.

Researchers suggest that without oxytocin, we wouldn't want to perform acts of generosity as we would lack empathy and find it nearly impossible to form strong bonds of trust, loyalty, or friendship. It is because of oxytocin that we enjoy being with other humans (the ones we like) and feel a sense of connectedness to those around us.

I've attempted to keep the science simple regarding the impact you have on the brain chemistry and subsequent performance of the people you work with. The evidence for giving people what they CRAVE is irrefutable. When people are recognized, they receive boosts in dopamine, serotonin, and oxytocin, which all work together to activate pleasure centers in our brains, helping us to feel more enthused about work and building a sense of pride and belonging. All of this drives motivation, stronger performance, and accelerated results over time.

When people are recognized, they receive boosts in dopamine, serotonin, and oxytocin, which all work together to activate pleasure centers in our brains.

THREESOME OF BRAIN CHEMICALS THAT GIVE US WHAT WE CRAVE			
CHEMICAL	DOPAMINE	SEROTONIN	OXYTOCIN
PRIMARY FEELING	pleasure	mood	trust
TRIGGERED BY	making progress	sense of pride	connectedness with others

Believers Make It a Top Priority to Accelerate Results

Not because it feels good to do it (although you should absolutely expect that benefit to materialize), but because it truly accelerates results. Recognition Results Doubters have not invested the time to truly explore the ability to accelerate outcomes. I can't say this enough: The Ultimate Habit's primary objective is about seeing, recognizing, and encouraging the kind of results your organization needs to be successful. I am not assuming this idea is obvious at first. And even if it is, you should not assume that this concept is obvious to everyone on your team and throughout your management ranks. If it were, effective employee recognition would be way more pervasive in your organization and throughout our society, we wouldn't continue to suffer from low employee engagement, and more organizations would be thriving due to better customer experiences.

The best way to ensure way more believers than doubters is to focus on the business results you want more of. So, let's do that together throughout the remainder of this book!

The Right Thing to Do, Real ROI, or Both?

When it comes to making an investment in employee recognition, I often hear two distinctly different perspectives from leaders. About 50 percent are those I refer to as the "feel-gooders." They have plans to implement an employee recognition program because it's simply the "right thing to do." They've seen the research, they know the humanistic benefits, and they are tasked by others in the organization to put a new program in place or try to fix an old, ineffective effort. These leaders are primarily motivated by the "soft" side of employee recognition and how it makes people feel.

The other 50 percent may also be interested in the soft, altruistic, and humanistic benefits of recognizing employees, but they won't truly "believe" unless they can see the return on investment (ROI). These individuals are more willing to challenge assumptions about the budget to be spent and whether it makes sense strategically.

I am not suggesting that one way of looking at recognition is good and another is bad. However, in the Recognition Is the Accelerator Model that follows, we will help you get laser-focused on the ROI side of recognition. Why? Because recognition is the "right thing to do," but without ROI it is very difficult to justify investing the dollars and time it takes (even if it is only a few minutes a week) to make strategically recognizing employees a management habit.

Aren't We Just Being Manipulative?

Look, there is no doubt that strategically recognizing employees is a terrific way to get more people to do what you want them to do. And it is because of this that some leaders get caught up thinking that they are being manipulative, especially when you begin to tie in a focus on business results. Some say, "It feels like we are being self-serving." From my experience, it's only manipulative if you are not genuine in your recognition, not because you are being strategic in considering what outcomes you want to see more of. It's manipulative when you don't really care about showing respect and helping others see the purpose and importance of what they do. It's manipulative if you don't really care about strengthening the relationship you have with those you work with. And, if you don't care or are not genuine, people can usually see right through you.

Zeroing in on the attitudes, activities, and experiences employees demonstrate that accelerate results is a far cry from being manipulative. In fact, some might argue it's called good management!

What Results Do You Want to Accelerate?

Let's think about the business results you are accountable for in your work area. What are the first few that come to mind? Do the attitudes and actions of employees have an impact on them? If so, then you have results to accelerate.

The table that follows has a list of suggested business results organized into a few industry categories. Let's do an exercise to document the results you'd like to see accelerated in your organization with the power of recognition. Begin by choosing the industry that most closely matches your organization. Next, review the list of results for that industry and see which ones apply. Make sure to review the other industries to see if any of them have results that are of high priority to you.

MANUFACTURING & DISTRIBUTION

- Fewer quality issues
- Increased productivity
- Better on-time delivery
- Fewer safety incidents
- Decreased insurance costs
- Increased employee retention
- Less lost time due to injury or illness

RETAIL & HOSPITALITY

- Improved customer retention
- Increased customer acquisition
- Fewer complaints
- Lower employee turnover
- Less employee absenteeism
- Improved satisfaction and loyalty

PROFESSIONAL SERVICES

- Increased average sale per client
- Greater client retention
- More referrals
- Increased cross-selling and up-selling
- Fewer quality issues
- Decreased employee absenteeism
- Less time to fill a job

HEALTH CARE

- Improved patient satisfaction
- Increased quantity of patients
- Fewer patient complaints
- Increased program participation
- Improved quality of care outcomes
- Decreased employee turnover/ absenteeism
- Fewer safety issues/incident reports

List the business results you want to accelerate:

1.

2.

3.

4.

5.

Your list is important. You will come back to it later in this book. In "Part 3: Mastering the Ultimate Habit," you will connect your strategic recognition efforts to these results. Once you adopt the Ultimate Habit, you can inspire other leaders to accelerate these business results in addition to results that are important to their work area.

THE RECOGNITION IS THE ACCELERATOR™ MODEL

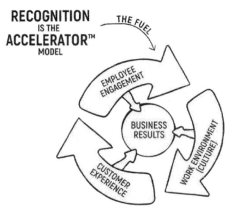

Our premise thus far has been quite simple: Demonstrating the Ultimate Habit of strategically recognizing employees fuels the work environment with what people CRAVE, which accelerates business results. Some leaders are natural believers; some are Recognition Results Doubters who need to clearly see the ROI to make the investment in building recognition as a leadership habit. And some think they are already doing recognition but are unware that they are not really providing what people CRAVE, mostly because their efforts are too infrequent or are not genuine or strategic enough.

The Accelerated Model Defined

According to the dictionary, accelerants are substances used to accelerate a process (such as the spreading of a fire). Scientists use them to speed up chemical reactions in lab experiments in order to achieve results more quickly.

Recognition is the fuel that accelerates employee engagement, the work culture, and the customer experience. Together, all three of these accelerated outcomes profoundly impact the business results you want more of.

10 Minutes by Friday™ Drives 150 Percent Increase in Employee Recognition

Patrick is the EVP of store operations for a large retailer. His company has nearly 100,000 employees, of which about 10,000 are managers, and more than 4,000 stores. Prior to Patrick's arrival at this organization, they had invested a significant amount of money and time rolling out a social recognition platform (an online portal for sharing kudos, thank-yous, and stories of success) only to find that over the first two years a mere 17 percent of the workforce were appreciated and recognized for living their values. Not exactly accelerating-results-type activity, and Patrick knew this.

My first encounter with this retailer's leadership team was one year before Patrick took the role of running store operations. I brought up the potential challenge of getting managers and the workforce to use this platform, but my concerns were met with deaf ears and an attitude of "We've got this. We've partnered with a vendor who is helping us to build a culture of appreciation."

After two years of relatively dismal recognition activity, I got the call I'd been waiting for. "Can you help us make recognition more pervasive throughout our workforce?" My response was, "Let's do this! But let's start with the business results you want most and first focus on the top one thousand leaders you want to lead the way. And let's get them to commit to 10 Minutes by Friday! Ten minutes to simply stop and think about an opportunity to recognize someone." The goal was to consider whether a recognizable moment happened that would be good to share, not only to provide that individual or team with what they CRAVE, but also to spread best practices for others to learn from.

The results they wanted to accelerate for the biggest impact on overall sales and profitability included:
1. Increase employee engagement
2. Increase customer satisfaction and loyalty
3. Decrease customer complaints
4. Decrease theft, both employee and customer (referred to as "shrink" in the industry)
5. Decrease safety incidents and associated insurance costs

Over the next sixty days, approximately one thousand top field leaders were taken through the Ultimate Habit process that is covered in Part 3 of this book (patience … you'll be there very soon). Each leader was introduced to the concept of 10 Minutes by Friday as a discipline for thinking about and sharing examples of employees "living the values." In addition, careful attention was paid to the business results they wanted to accelerate.

What happened next? Well, within two months, use of their recognition platform increased from 17 percent to 42 percent—a nearly 150 percent increase. Even more impressive were the accelerated results uncovered in the following year:

- Employee engagement rose 24 percent in areas where leaders provided optimal recognition.
- Customer complaints fell 38 percent.
- Employee and customer theft decreased. A strong correlation between recognition activity, the workforce demonstrating the values, and the impact on shrink—clearly showing that people who received recognition were more likely to act in the organization's best interest, resulting in less theft and product damage.
- Customer accidents decreased 32 percent. According to one leader, "More focus through our recognition effort on the safety and care for customers has improved awareness of things that could cause accidents."

Were these results exclusively triggered by increased recognition? Of course not. But a call from Patrick provided an intriguing insight. He said, "You can certainly accelerate results without doing a great job recognizing employees. You can also start a fire without matches and lighter fluid, but doing so is way more difficult. Strategically recognizing employees is the fuel that ignites business results faster."

Let's dive into the Recognition Is the Accelerator Model so you can begin to think more about ways to make recognition more strategic and pervasive throughout your organization.

ACCELERATE EMPLOYEE ENGAGEMENT

Employee Engagement: Everyone Wants More of It

An engaged employee is one who is both motivated and committed to act in the best interest of your organization. And, if you want more of them, you must give employees more of what they CRAVE. What Patrick said about strategically recognizing employ-

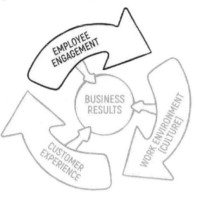

ees being the fuel that ignites business results is also true for employee engagement. Yes, you can achieve certain business results with disengaged employees, but doing so is way more expensive.

> *An engaged employee is both motivated and committed to act in the best interest of your organization.*

Employees Are Not Your Greatest Asset!

I love to share this statement with leaders from up on the stage all the way down to small groups around a conference room table. Each and every time I get the same suspicious, yet curious, response. Their looks say, "What do you mean? Our people are super important and without them we can't possibly be at our best for customers." Usually, this is followed by an awkward silence where leaders try to make sense of a concept that seems contrary to what they've heard people say for as long as they can remember. To make my point, I share a slightly different perspective: *"The right employees who are engaged are your greatest asset."* Then, I share the startling statistic that two-thirds of Americans are not engaged at work.[38] "So," I ask, "if two-thirds of your workforce is not engaged, how can they possibly be your greatest asset? They are not. The one-third who are engaged … they are your greatest asset."

I shared this example in my previous books: *Achieve Brand Integrity* back in 2007 and *ENGAGED!* in 2013. And over the years, leaders' reactions have changed. While at first the question sparks suspicion and curiosity, many are now familiar with the research I share because of the numerous blogs, articles, and studies on the topic and, therefore, are aware of—and in many cases witnessing firsthand—just how expensive the lack of engagement is. Conversations about employee engagement happen more and more in strategic planning meetings. It comes as no surprise that almost every organization on this planet wants to have more engaged employees.

Lack of engagement is expensive!

The "want" is there; the results are not. The research reminds us year after year that we have an employee engagement crisis that costs our society billions of dollars a year in lost productivity and less-than-ideal customer experiences.

The Engagement Crisis Is Really an Energy Crisis!

The energy crisis I am referring to is probably not what you think of when you hear the term. I am referring to the lack of energy you get from the workforce around you. When an employee joins your organization, there is a "deal" made that assumes the organization will live up to an expectation as an employer of choice and the employee will bring their time, talent, and effort to the job. That's the deal! However, when employees don't feel respected for the work they do or lose sight of the purpose, meaning, and importance of their work, they soon feel as if they are getting a raw deal. They don't explicitly say, "I am not getting what I CRAVE," but subconsciously, that's what they are feeling. Instead, they complain about people ("I can't stand my boss"), their income ("I don't make enough money to deal with this place"), or customers ("They drive me crazy").

What happens next is where the crisis begins ... they start to withhold their energy. But this is the energy you are "buying." You are paying for it in their weekly paycheck. Since the employee feels a bit cheated, as if the organization or their manager doesn't support their efforts, guess what? That effort (energy) goes out the open window like the heat in your house on a wintry day.

In an evidence-based research study, Robert Eisenberger, Glenn P. Malone, and William D. Presson proposed that when an organization shows it values employees' work and contributions (the difference they make), it leads to improvements in psychological well-being and employee performance, while at the same time reducing absenteeism and turnover. Hence ... more energy. They conclude that leaders who show their support provide significant benefits to employees and the employer, saying "employees are more likely to be emotionally committed to the organization, inclined to increase performance and less likely to be absent or leave the organization."[39] They go on to state also that providing employees this little extra support increases happiness and reduces stress. Which obviously leads to more energy.

Recognition done strategically provides that catalyst for capturing more of the energy your organization has already purchased. When employees are asked, "How does receiving recognition and rewards at work make you feel?"

- 81% say it makes them feel more committed
- 79% say it makes them work harder
- 78% say it helps them be more productive[40]

Conclusion: If you want to capture more energy—more motivation and commitment from employees who work harder and contribute to increased productivity—then recognize people more.

If only it were that simple.

Paper Forms, Spreadsheets, and Rewards Catalogs … Oh My!

In 2002, I set out to eradicate employee disengagement—or at least make a meaningful, positive difference in the world. I would help organizations create more alignment, motivation, and commitment among all employees, managers, and executives on what it takes to live an organization's core values. I knew if I could at least do that, I would be helping to make better places to work.

It was fall and my company had recently completed a project with a sign manufacturing company with about one hundred employees. We worked with their leadership to define a new set of values to support their mission statement. At the conclusion of the project, we brainstormed ways to reinforce and remind the workforce of the values and how to live them. The CEO (Stephen) said, "In the past, I've offered people an on-the-spot bonus of $20 if they can recite the mission." I thought to myself … *That is ridiculous. Who cares if people can memorize the mission? Stephen needs his workforce to live the values.* Stephen could tell by the look on my face that I had something to say. I took a deep breath, and calmly and respectfully shared my opinion: "Stephen, your goal is to have people 'live the mission,' not memorize it. You need to get people talking about it, keeping it top of mind in ways that influence the way they think, speak, and act around here."

It was at that moment that our first "Living the Values Employee Recognition Program" was born. It was quite simple in concept, yet I must admit, quite difficult to execute. We quickly learned it was a flawed approach that would not work, especially for larger organizations.

Here was the idea we deployed: Each employee could nominate a colleague for "living the values." They simply filled out a small card, which we stationed strategically around the office and shop floor. On the card, they wrote in the name of who they were nominating (recognizing) with a short description of what the person did to live the values. Then they submitted the card to the central office, where it was passed on to a supervisor to approve. Once approved, it went back to the central office for coding into a spreadsheet and points were awarded to both the person who nominated someone and the person who was nominated. Employees could redeem their points for merchandise in a catalog (yes, a paper catalog).

We tracked everything in an Excel spreadsheet. Sounds great … right? Not really. The problem seems obvious now. Even with minimal activity, let's say a few recognitions each week, the day-to-day management was cumbersome and no one wanted to own it. And, you know what surprised me? Most managers didn't even want to participate. The program limped along for a few years but never got the momentum we envisioned.

Needless to say, we stopped the program. It was so challenging to manage and had little impact on the workforce, not to mention on improving employee engagement. But I couldn't get out of my mind how powerful this program COULD be ...

If You Build It, They Will Come—Unless They Don't

In 2005, my firm, Brand Integrity, built the first online social recognition portal. I know that may sound crazy, but it's true. Frankly, if others had it, I would not have ventured into building one. Brand Integrity was a culture consulting organization. What business did we have getting into the software business? But, I couldn't be idle in my quest to make better places to work.

At the time, I had never heard of Facebook, and the idea of a social platform to communicate successes and recognize employees was truly a foreign idea. But we believed it was one worth pursuing. So we did. We turned our paper-based, Excel-managed idea into an automated online program designed to fuel what people CRAVE.

What I didn't realize back then was that our mission to create more engagement would also require that we help organizations create better leaders and that this could be done through the habit of strategic recognition. (We will dive deep into the topic of becoming a more trusted leader in Part 3 when we get into the Ultimate Habit process.) At the time, we knew we needed to build something that would capture the moment an employee "lived the brand" and ensure it could be shared with their manager and others throughout the workforce who could learn from it. We built the program so each submitted recognition (the word "post" was not yet mainstream) linked the action to a core value and the business results that it had the most impact on. Employees simply picked from a short list provided. The recognition was reviewed by a manager and then shared in a centralized feed for others to learn from. We designed it this way knowing that doing so would help people feel respected and better understand the impact of their work. The program also enabled participants to get points for both recognizing others and being recognized. Those points could be redeemed for an Amazon gift card right through our system. (Of course, the entire process of ordering the gift card was originally done manually in Brand Integrity's back office.)

In late 2005, the first version of our software was built and we naively, yet passionately, began to set up meetings with potential clients. Surely they were going to embrace the concept, sign up, and launch it across their organizations, right? Not so fast. I wish I recorded some of the meetings we had with prospective clients. Many of them thought we were crazy.

In fact, time after time, our product was met with skepticism: "Won't people game the system, recognizing each other just to get points?" To which I replied, "No, they won't, but if it does happen, so what? As long as they are capturing examples of people 'living the brand,' you will create more alignment and engagement in your organization. You will get more people learning about and doing things the way you want them done." Our logic prevailed to a certain extent, but what we learned was that many organizations were not convinced they could get their managers to use it. And they were right.

We added a few clients each year for several years. A few did very well with the program, clearly accelerating the business outcomes we've been thinking about and referring to so far in this book. They were able to see tangible increases in employee engagement, decreases in unwanted employee turnover, fewer quality issues, and improvements in customer experiences and loyalty scores. In these cases, employees were clearly getting more of what they CRAVED from the positive recognition activity, yet several clients were not seeing the same accelerated results. And the reasons were quite evident. Today, we would label these clients as the "set-it-and-forget-it" type, organizations that were enamored with the idea of having an online tool for proactively recognizing employees and doing so in a "peer-to-peer" fashion. What separated out the clients who successfully accelerated results was that in addition to the peer-to-peer mentality, they also realized that the program needed to be led by management to maximize success—meaning leaders actually had to do recognitions online and share examples in the offline world as well. As I shared earlier, this is not a natural skill for most managers. While deep down inside, they know it is the right thing to do, making it a habit was not so easy.

The Engagement Industry Gets Bigger, But Not Better

These days, Brand Integrity's innovative employee engagement platform is now one of hundreds (and hundreds may be an understatement) of social recognition programs being offered across the globe. Social media has become mainstream in our personal lives and at work, too. If it hasn't become prevalent in your workplace, given the generational changes we've covered, it will very soon.

Across our client base, we continue to see how certain companies accelerate results, and others ... well ... don't. We've found that much of the success is driven by technology use.

After our first eight years into this journey of deploying recognition in an online portal, Brand Integrity decided to do some research to learn more about what was going on in the marketplace and within our own client base. We wanted to explore the reasons some clients excelled where others didn't. We retained a branding and market research firm to conduct an extensive study that included approximately five hundred interviews. Linda and Ryan were the two primary researchers who spent several months conducting the interviews to understand what was happening in the market. A few of the interviews were with leaders within our client base, but most were with people in the market who were investing in and leading employee engagement improvement efforts.

In these interviews, Linda and Ryan looked to uncover attitudes and issues with respect to employee engagement (specifically, the efforts to put the power of recognition to work to make improvement a reality), how buying decisions were made and later rationalized, and what aspects of an organization's employee engagement efforts had the most significant impact for customers.

What they found was, at the time, both unexpected, yet insightful. My leadership team and I gathered around the conference room table in anticipation of the findings they would present. Linda started it off:

> *Organizations have "wicked problems" when it comes to engaging their people. Don't think for a minute that employee recognition is going to solve all of these problems. Certainly, it can help. But it has to be done the right way. Doing something isn't better than doing nothing. The wrong something can actually make things much worse. What organizations don't want is a token culture of recognition or engagement. People don't want shallow*

> *campaigns that will never carve out a competitive advantage, inspire pride, and reduce stress. Gift cards are easier, but they will never increase the motivations of people who want the kind of change that actually changes things.*

Linda was referring to set-it-and-forget-it programs. She explained that half-baked attempts at showing appreciation don't provide what people CRAVE; in addition, most employees see right through them: They turn off more people than they turn on.

Regarding culture change, their research highlighted that it is all about mindsets and behaviors and that throwing technology at the problem simply won't work. They concluded:

> *Culture change is all in people's heads. It happens in employees' minds. Changes in technology (such as a social recognition platform), programs, or policies just won't cut it. You have to help leaders form new mindsets and behaviors and foster a revived sense of duty to achieve business goals, as the goals being achieved are what create job security and opportunity for personal development. Achieving goals and developing personally is what speaks to people's hearts; this is what drives them to sustain change. A new reality forms inside the most successful organizations and that reality always begins with a mindset shift.*

Technology Alone Won't Solve the Engagement Crisis

Flash forward another four years and we arrive at today. The insights shared by Linda and Ryan are way more obvious, as we see a growing number of organizations attempt to throw technology at the problem of the employee engagement crisis while not successfully engaging managers with their role in fueling the environment with what people CRAVE.

Recently, I was in Fresno, California, speaking at an event for business owners, leaders, and frontline managers all interested in learning about the Ultimate Habit and the 10 Minutes by Friday Challenge.

I shared the definition of employee engagement that I shared here with you: Engaged equals motivation plus commitment to act in the best interest of your organization. I asked for confirmation that they could all benefit from a bit more engagement from their workforce and received a lot of head nods. I then shared a little evidence I knew would spark emotion—a couple stats indicating that the great majority of workers simply don't qualify as engaged:

- 2/3 of employees are not engaged at work[41]
- 88% of employees go home at the end of the day and don't think their organization cares about them as people[42]

After sharing evidence like this I tend to get fired up on the stage. So, next I asked for a show of hands: "How many of you work in an organization that has invested in or is currently investing in an employee engagement strategy or initiative?" I hadn't planned to ask this question. I had never asked it before. It popped out of my mouth in the heat of the moment. Instantly, almost every single hand in the audience went up. I was a bit surprised. I improvised:

> *Keep your hands up and look around the room. Just about every hand is up. You are truly a representation of organizations across America. With so many organizations investing in engagement initiatives and many implementing engagement technologies that make big promises of driving stronger employee performance, how in the world can we still be suffering from so much disengagement in the workplace?*

My question was met with hundreds of blank stares. I had this audience right where I wanted them:

> *The engagement industry keeps getting bigger, but it's not getting any better. Throwing technology at the employee engagement program* doesn't work! *I am "guilty as charged"—my company's early attempts at deploying a social recognition platform didn't lead to the results we wanted. And that was our fault back then. But there is no*

excuse for organizations today who truly want to improve culture. You can't do the set-it-and-forget-it thing and expect to achieve meaningful results.

After that day in Fresno I decided to dig deeper into this idea about corporate spending to improve engagement. What I found was quite interesting.

Let's revisit the employee engagement chart. Only this time let's view the past five years and add a second dimension—the corporate spending on technology in America to increase employee engagement. It is estimated that in 2013, $3.7 billion was invested, increasing 30 percent the following year. By the end of 2017 the estimated investment was nearly $8 billion.[43] That's more than a 100 percent increase in spending over five years while the engagement level has fluctuated only a few percentage points. Personally, I find this gap to be outrageous! And you should too. It's unreasonable that organizations spend billions of dollars on HR technology and tools yet seem to receive so little return on the investment.

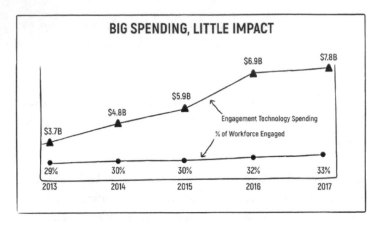

Why is this happening? The answer is simple. Leaders tend not to use the technology, at least not in the intended way or often enough. Technology alone does not improve engagement and work culture. This might sound quite obvious. Intellectually it makes sense. It's common sense. You wouldn't invest in a CRM system or sales management tool (for example, Salesforce.com) and expect that your customer relationships would improve and sales would go up solely based on the investment made in software. But we tend to do this a bit more when it comes to HR technology. Just because you've put in a new hiring system with ideal interview questions, or performance software with goal management, or a recognition system for sharing successes does not mean that leaders will ask the right questions, manage effectively to goals, or give people what they CRAVE by strategically recognizing them. What is apparent in the market is that, in most cases … they won't.

According to Steve Smith, partner at the Starr Conspiracy, a leading global human capital management research and marketing consultancy:

> *What we are seeing in our research is that user adoption of HR technology is a complete failure. Organizations are not getting the ROI promised. By the time they figure it out, the HR leader has moved on, a new HR leader comes in and says, "It's a technology problem. Let's replace it and try something else," and the cycle continues.*

Earlier I bragged a little about our clients and how they are witnessing nearly three times the engagement level of the average organization. Across a dozen industries we serve, engagement levels over the past five years average out to 91 percent, with 56 percent of employees highly engaged and 35 percent qualifying as moderately engaged. This is across all of our clients. You might be thinking that some industries must be quite different from others. Not so. The lowest-scoring industry is heavy manufacturing and, even in this setting, engagement hovers around 89 percent.

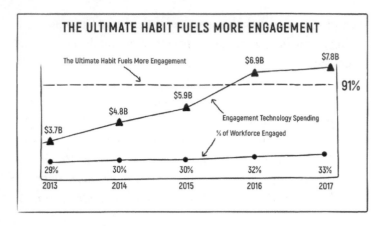

What are these leading organizations doing differently? Is there some type of magic fairy dust? Not at all. What they are doing is inspiring leaders to make it a habit to use the technology investment to create the environment where engagement thrives.

Thinking about this another way … they are not trying to force motivation on people.

The Big Fallacy … You Can't Motivate People

Consider how many times we've fallen victim to the fallacy that it is our jobs as leaders to motivate the workforce. We've all heard the comments, and many of us have even said, "I can't seem to motivate Stacy" or "Jimmy doesn't seem to want to work hard and I don't know what else I can do to light a fire under him." As leaders, we can't help but think it is our job to motivate people and that doing so will be sustainable over time.

Motivation is within us as humans at work (and at home), and it is up to each of us to determine if we are going to tap into our reserve of motivation each day. We decide if we will speak positively about the organization, coworkers, and customers, and we determine if we will provide that little extra discretionary effort.

So, if it is not your job as a leader to motivate others, if the truth is that you can't beg for or bribe for more motivation, then what is your job?

To answer this question, think back to what I shared earlier about how Edward Deci and Richard Ryan pioneered new frontiers in the study of motivation. They started by changing the question from "How can people motivate others?" to "How can people create the conditions where others will motivate themselves?"

Using this new frame of reference as our guide, we can conclude that it's the job of the leader to **create the environment** where people will tap into more of their personal motivation. This is more than a slight change of wording. This is an entirely different concept that puts the onus on you, the leader, to make sure your workplace is set up to give people what they CRAVE!

It's the leader's job to create the environment where people will tap into more of their personal motivation.

ACCELERATE THE WORK ENVIRONMENT

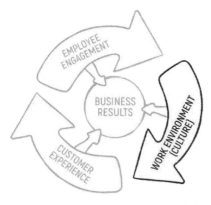

As I've shared over and over thus far, employee engagement statistics have remained at the same low rate, with two-thirds of the workplace not engaged. But what if we separate out management? How engaged are managers at work?

Recently, an exhaustive and somewhat shocking study on management engagement was released. To my knowledge, this study is the first of its kind to look at management engagement. And the results are surprising! Management engagement is only slightly better than employee engagement:

- 35% of managers are engaged
- 51% of managers are not engaged
- 14% of managers are actively disengaged[44]

How in the world can we expect to improve workforce engagement when managers themselves are so challenged to get what they CRAVE? And because of this, many are disengaged, which means they may not be willing to give the organization that little extra discretionary effort or may not be speaking positively about the organization or the people in it. Additionally, they may not be planning on staying with the organization and may be investing their time and energy looking for their next opportunity.

The authors of this study logically point out that "until organizations can increase their percentage of engaged managers, they have little hope of increasing their percentage of engaged employees."[45]

Here is where the great big opportunity I referred to comes to fruition. CRAVE applies to all humans at work, not only employees on the front line. It is just as important for managers to feel respected for the work they do and understand the purpose and meaning of their work. It's just as important for managers to form strong bonds and relationships at work and understand how their behavior impacts employees and the organization as a whole.

"Until organizations can increase their percentage of engaged managers, they have little hope of increasing their percentage of engaged employees."[46]

We've witnessed over and over how management engagement increases when employee recognition is done consistently and strategically is led by managers throughout the ranks. So, let's dive into the power of recognition, what it is, and how it can be done strategically.

When You Give It, You Get It

O.C. Tanner produced one of the biggest global, peer-to-peer research studies ever conducted that focused on how doing employee recognition—in ways that show respect and highlight the importance of people's work—impacts employee engagement. Their findings below clearly show that not only do we get what we CRAVE when we're recognized, we also get it when we recognize others. And one might argue this is especially true for managers.

- 30% of employees who said they "never/rarely" give recognition are engaged
- 46% of employees who said they "sometimes" give recognition are engaged
- 66% of employees who said they "often" give recognition are engaged
- 81% of employees who said they "always" give recognition are engaged[47]

The study reveals an incredible 170 percent increase (30 percent to 81 percent) in employee engagement between those who proactively recognize others and those who don't.

We get what we CRAVE when we recognize others for doing good work.

Focus on the 20 Percent Momentum Builders, Not the 20 Percent Who Spread Poison

Allow me to share with you a conversation I had over breakfast with the CEO (Alex) of a professional services firm with 4,300 employees spread across offices throughout the Northeast. Alex is in her third year leading the implementation of a social recognition program where managers were introduced to the Ultimate Habit as a strategic management discipline, with an investment of 10 Minutes by Friday as a personal goal. Alex shared what researchers refer to as the Diffusion of Innovations theory, which seeks to explain how, why, and at what rate new ideas and technology spread. In addition, this is a terrific example of how a little bit of effort, 10 Minutes by Friday for instance, can lead to significant momentum, decrease skepticism, and overall affect the acceleration of results. All while providing employees—and managers—what they CRAVE!

When a group of leaders is asked to change their beliefs and behaviors (in Alex's case, to begin thinking of recognition as a strategic management discipline, that is, a habit they should invest in building), all the coaching and training in the world usually turns out to have little impact. That is, until enough early adopters begin to apply the discipline.

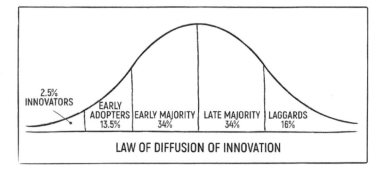

Diffusion of Innovation theory states that 2.5 percent of people will be the Innovators who champion the initial change. Next come the Early Adopters at 13.5 percent—these are the very willing participants who, in most cases, have been seeking this type of opportunity to think and do something different. These first two sections house those who will most likely begin to adopt the habit of strategically recognizing employees if given the right tools and training.

In the middle and back end of the curve, some convincing is necessary to change beliefs and spark action. This starts with the Early Majority (34 percent)—those who tend to get on board as soon as they see initial evidence that doing so is in their best interest. They only need a little convincing. Next come the Late Majority (34 percent), who also tend to buy in, but not as quickly (they need plenty of evidence over time to be convinced). Last are the Laggards at 16 percent. These leaders will most likely never buy in regardless of how much proof you provide. They are not open to a mindset shift and have zero interest or can't possibly see the need to alter their behaviors.

According to Everett M. Rogers, author of *Diffusion of Innovations*, "An important factor regarding the adoption rate of an innovation is its compatibility with the values, beliefs, and past experiences of individuals in the social system."[48] For our purposes, the heart of the diffusion process consists of other leaders modeling and imitating the Innovators and Early Adopters who, once they reach a critical mass of 20 percent or more, will spark larger segments of the management group to follow suit. After enough repetition, positive reinforcement, and time, you should expect the ideal beliefs, attitudes, and behaviors to be adopted by the majority. Before you know it, a critical mass has evolved with a common mindset that fuels the culture of appreciation and strategic recognition that truly does accelerate business outcomes.

When talking with Alex, I commented that in the first two years of the program more than 50 percent of their managers were already doing a very good job taking a few minutes each week to think about an employee's success in living the values and/or having an impact on business results (the 10 Minutes by Friday Challenge). Half of the managers in Alex's organization did at least one strategic recognition per month in their online social recognition platform.

Alex shared how recognition was clearly having an impact on their employee engagement and customer loyalty scores. She noted that more than 80 percent of her workforce actively participated in their employee recognition program and overall employee engagement was up by more than 30 percent over the full three-year period. Their main service division, which housed nearly one-third of the workforce, witnessed an increase in employee engagement of 52 percent. This improvement helped accelerate their overall customer loyalty metrics by 68 percent. And, to Alex's pleasant surprise, both of these outstanding improvements were powered by a 111 percent increase in the amount of employee recognition in their employee engagement platform.

The evidence of acceleration was powerful and very important to Alex as she witnessed that sharing the connections with her management helped remind them of the impact taking a few minutes to recognize successes had on their customer experience. That translated to fewer customer complaints, improved brand image in the markets they served, and overall stronger sales.

What did this mean from a financial perspective? Well, they finished their most profitable year of the past twenty, increasing their operating margin 4.6 percent from just three years before. Not an insignificant amount, given that this led to more than $100 million in profit.

Obviously, their employee recognition activity can't take claim for all of these results. Lots of economic and operational impacts influence profit margin. However, when Alex was asked if it had a strong influence, her response was, "Of course it does!"

What Alex and her executive leadership team were able to do in a few short years was get many of the Early Majority and Late Majority to come on board. At the time of this writing, approximately 53 percent were successfully doing the 10 Minutes by Friday Challenge with the goal of at least one strategic recognition shared per month.

I can imagine what you might be thinking and asking: "That's it? All they had to do was one per month posted to an online site for others to learn from? One example in a month that helps fuel the cravings for an employee or group of employees?"

Yes, that is it. That is the recipe you will learn in "Part 3: Mastering the Ultimate Habit." As you will see, it is quite simple and easy to do—but also even easier not to do, which is why getting 53 percent is quite an achievement. This does not mean that the other managers did not take the time to capture and share successes—many did—with the total participation from management at 74 percent over the same time period. What's different is that the other 47 percent didn't make it a habit. This means they may not be doing strategic recognition consistently and often enough. They may be missing the opportunity to give people what they CRAVE, diminishing productivity, increasing costs, and making it more difficult to achieve the desired business results. As stated previously, managers also CRAVE feeling respected and having an understanding of the purpose of their role and the difference they make. While not embracing the Ultimate Habit may seem the easier option, they are not getting their cravings filled as much as they could, therefore diminishing their impact and success as a leader.

> *Managers also CRAVE feeling respected and having an understanding of the purpose of their role and the difference they make.*

I reminded Alex that when we began this journey a few years back, we stated that about 20 percent would be on board immediately (the Early Adopters), but as many as 15 or 20 percent (the Laggards) may not ever get on board. Alex said:

> *You were right on target. In fact, the 20 percent were more than just laggards. They were poison! Constantly chirping about how the program was a waste of time, would never work to improve results, or that they simply didn't have time given their workload. But something interesting happened over the past year—the spreading of poison decreased and decreased a lot. There is so much momentum and buy-in now that they are "at risk" when*

> *spreading their poison. Others simply don't agree with*
> *them. They are at risk of looking as bad as they sound.*

What Alex and her executive team discovered is exactly what I believe you will encounter as well.

- Making employee recognition a habit is simple and easy to do. But, it is also even easier not to do, which is why a habit must be formed (Part 3).
- As momentum builds, and more employees get what they CRAVE, more managers will begin to build the confidence and form the habit.
- Managers will soon realize they too get what they CRAVE—respect for being a good leader and a feeling of purpose and importance in their role as they have a more positive impact on employees.
- A portion of your managers may never get on board. But over time they will spread less poison as doing so becomes risky when they clearly see they are the minority.

Some Managers Are Jerks

Robert Sutton is the author of *Good Boss, Bad Boss*. In his book, Sutton reveals what the best and worst bosses do to create workplaces where employee engagement thrives. Most bosses (and their followers) aspire to become (or work for) an all-around great boss, he writes, somebody with the skill and grit to inspire superior work, commitment, and dignity among their charges. People who don't take the time to recognize successes and share them are jerks. And often they don't even know it. Sutton encourages his readers to "build 'jerk-free' workplaces," going on to say, "I've worked with and been part of too many places where bosses spend endless hours preparing for evaluations but don't take even a few moments to make people feel appreciated."[49]

Sutton is correct. Some leaders are jerks and won't open their minds to the concept of giving people what they CRAVE. They simply don't (and maybe never will) see the positive impact fulfilling this craving can have on accelerating business results. However, keep in mind that while they are noisy (spreading poison), in most cases they are the minority.

The good news is that, as momentum builds and more and more leaders fuel the work environment with what people CRAVE, they also get their cravings filled and the poison dissipates over time.

Stress ... the Hidden Assassin

We have to stop ignoring the science and research. No, I'm not referring again to the decades of data on what causes motivation (or lack of) in the workplace. I am not referring to the constant proliferation of data on how disengaged people are at work. What I am referring to is the decades of research on what causes stress in the workplace, which only adds to the motivation and engagement challenges.

109

Stress is defined as "a state of mental or emotional strain or tension resulting from adverse or very demanding circumstances."[50] Unfortunately, we have plenty in our workplace today, costing the economy upward of $300 billion a year in lost productivity and insurance costs.[51]

What is causing this stress? Chances are, it's you! (And me too.) Now please don't be offended. I'm just playing the odds here based on the immense research on the subject of stress at work:

- 3 out of 4 employees say their boss is the worst and most stressful part of their job.[52]
- 65% of employees say they'd take a new boss over a pay raise.[53]
- On a given workday, an estimated 1 million workers are absent due to stress.[54]
- Employees with managers they don't like are 60% more likely to suffer a heart attack.[55]

It is clear that "the boss" has a gigantic impact on the level of stress in the workplace. So, here is my thesis: Giving people what they CRAVE will decrease workplace stress.

Is it safe to assume that in many cases, maybe even most, if a manager does a good job investing a few minutes each week to stop and recognize a success, showing employees they respect them and the work they are doing, that an employee will feel a bit less stress and instead feel more pride, work harder, and like their boss a little more?

We all know the answer to this loaded question is ... YES!

Giving people what they CRAVE will decrease workplace stress.

Let's not let stress be the hidden assassin at work any longer. As a leader, you have the power to make a positive impact every day. Of course, you can do this many ways in how you manage and lead your team. I am not suggesting that the Ultimate Habit of strategically recognizing employees is the only strategy. However, it sure is a simple, very powerful, way to ensure people get what they CRAVE, while improving the relationship your team has with you as a leader.

You Can't Stop the Raging River

Even with all of this evidence and logic, some may still feel as if taking on the responsibility of doing the Ultimate Habit is a daunting task they simply don't have the time for. In reality, it will save time. Lots of time. Consider that 79 percent of people who leave their job report a lack of appreciation as the reason they left.[56] When people leave, especially those you don't want to leave, it costs you and everyone around you time (and money). Therefore, it's time to make the time!

If you are like most people today, you feel overwhelmed with too much to do and too little time.

I'll bet you create to-do lists, don't you? Leaders do this to stay focused and try to accomplish key objectives. And what happens once you get a few things checked off that list? What is waiting for you? That's right, a few more things to do. Sometimes you feel as though you'll never get caught up. I call this the Raging River of Responsibility and most leaders suffer from it. Like rapids coming down the river, your to-dos and high-priority tasks keep coming. You get a few done and more pop up. The Raging River of Responsibility does not end. Thinking so is ... wishful thinking. But, you can reprioritize and make the Ultimate Habit a must-do leadership skill in helping you to create the environment where more people will become more engaged. When you do, you will fuel the work environment with what employees CRAVE: more respect, a better understanding of purpose, and a stronger relationship with you—decreasing stress and *saving you time*.

I hate to belabor the point about "having the time" to do recognition and do it well. But I must because this is the number one excuse I hear over and over from managers at all levels. The evidence that giving employees what they CRAVE in order to influence motivation and improve performance is easy to understand and difficult to refute. From my experience, most leaders are not jerks, and they aren't failing to recognize employees because they don't believe in it. Instead, either they don't think of employee recognition as a strategic management discipline or they default to the idea that they don't have the time.

Throughout the remainder of this book, you will learn more about what to recognize people for and how to do it strategically and effectively. Together, we will diffuse the time bomb, the completely irrational excuse! My job as your guide is to continue to share examples that get you thinking about business results so you start to realize that the small amount of time invested in mastering the Ultimate Habit is the best time you spend.

Ten Minutes Drives Real ROI

A few years ago, I had the privilege of speaking about the Ultimate Habit to a group of fifty managers at a nursing home facility near Buffalo, New York. These managers led a workforce of about five hundred people. Their CEO, Jeff, stepped on stage that day feeling confident, yet also maybe a little insecure about what was about to take place. I'll explain his insecurity in a moment.

Jeff stepped up to introduce me to his managers. He said:

> *Our industry is suffering from too much employee turnover. We are not immune to it. We are holding steady at the industry average (about 40 percent). Our customer*

113

satisfaction scores have been flat for quite some time. In fact, they have not really changed a noticeable amount in the twenty-three years I have worked here. In addition, I've heard from many of you in the recent past that you feel overworked and underappreciated. Well, together, we will explore how we can change this.

At this point I thought Jeff was ready to introduce me, but he continued:

In the past year, we've redefined our organizational core values. We all know what they are and why they are important. But we seem to be challenged with knowing how to do them consistently. We are simply too inconsistent with how we live our values throughout our work culture and with our customers—the residents and family members who help care for them. We can change this, YOU can change this, and together we can become an even better place to work and live.

Here is what I am asking you to do: Commit to investing ten minutes each week to STOP, THINK about, and consider sharing an example of our core values in action. That's it! Take the time to consider whether you've witnessed an employee living our values and, if so, share it in our online recognition portal for the rest of us to see, appreciate, and learn from.

Next Jeff introduced me as the guy who would help them learn the Ultimate Habit of strategically recognizing employees, which I did over the next forty-five minutes. Jeff inspired them and then I stepped in to share the step-by-step approach that you will learn in Part 3.

What this organization achieved was nothing short of amazing when you think about the known challenges with trying to staff and manage a nursing home environment. It's a very difficult place to create engagement, to say the least. The work can be tiring, stressful, and thankless. At the same time, Jeff and his team of leaders proved that it can be emotionally rewarding when employees get what they CRAVE.

In the next twelve months, two-thirds of the leaders met the challenge of 10 Minutes by Friday, which led to 3,800 strategic, values-driven employee recognitions. And these were not just simple thank-yous; they were thoughtful stories (a few sentences to a full paragraph) that highlighted how the values were lived and the impact the person's actions had on the business results that mattered most. What was most impressive was that the majority (60 percent) were posted and shared by frontline staff who became more motivated and committed week after week. By the end of the first year, employee engagement scores increased by more than 125 percent and employee turnover decreased 12 percent. What was the impact of recognition on these business results? As it turns out, we found a 0.865 corre-lation between employee recognition activity and engagement scores. For those of you who are not statistics connoisseurs, this means Jeff and his team witnessed an incredibly strong connec-tion between strategically recognizing people (to provide what they CRAVE) and their level of motivation and commitment (engagement). Which obviously had a direct result on employee turnover.

I called up Jeff as soon as I saw these results. It was at this time that he confided in me about the insecurity he was feeling the day he introduced the 10 Minutes by Friday Challenge to his managers. Jeff said:

> *Gregg, when I proposed that ten-minute investment of time to my team of managers, I was not even sure if I could make it a habit. I promised them I would invest ten minutes each week and I was worried that might be too much to commit to. I knew going in that I suffered from the "I don't have time" syndrome that most use as an excuse. But, I have to tell you, after witnessing the posi-tive cultural impact, I don't know how anyone can justify not spending the time. A 12 percent drop in turnover is not an inconsequential amount. That saves us time and money. In addition, there are pockets where we are not doing recognition as well and suffer from the same head-aches as years past. In those areas, employee turnover*

has not changed and absenteeism is up, which means we have to cover more shifts and spend more money in overtime pay. And this is time consuming. Where we do recognition well, there is a palpable improvement in morale. It just feels different.

"A 12% drop in turnover is not an inconsequential amount. [It] saves time and money!"

I'll never forget the call with Jeff. I could hear in his voice how psyched he was to finally move the needle on accelerating his mission-critical business outcomes. And the beauty of it was ... he did so in a way that was saving him (and his managers) the most precious commodity—time!

One Year Later. Even Less Turnover and Happier Customers

Approximately one year later we connected again to pore over the results. It had only gotten better. Employee engagement had increased even further. They were now up to more than seven thousand captured recognitions in their employee engagement platform. Employee turnover dropped another two points to a 14 percent decrease. And, most exciting of all, those customer satisfaction scores that had not changed in the past twenty-three years were now up 20 percent.

Was employee recognition the only catalyst for these fantastically accelerated business results? No way. But was it the driving force? Absolutely! And they have the data to prove it!

Revisit the Business Results That Matter Most

Some of the challenges with not having enough of the right kind of recognition stem from not having the right mindset. With that said, let's not overcomplicate this. In the pages that follow, we will cover not only what to recognize for, but how to do it strategically so that you can truly accelerate the business results that matter most to you.

Let's revisit those desired results you took note of earlier on. Consider the organization-wide, department, or team goals you want to achieve. Think about the metrics that matter most to your work area. Next, you will begin to think about spotting activities and experiences that employees perform that help lead to these goals.

An Incomplete List of Ways to Strategically Recognize

Strategic recognition can appear in many forms and formats. The important thing is that it happens and happens in a genuine and timely fashion. How you recognize people will depend on:

- The effort level you witnessed.
- The impact on accelerating the desired business results.

- Existing employee recognition programs available in your organization.
- And in some cases, your own personal preference.

Below is a list of common ways to do employee recognition. Depending on your organization and what you are recognizing for, they will have varying degrees of impact. If your goal is to fulfill what people CRAVE and also keep people focused on accelerating business results, then, from my experience, the ideal way to recognize is to make it personal, tie it to specific values, and ensure it is shared with others. I've broken down the list into what I've witnessed as high impact versus lower impact from the perspective of giving people what they CRAVE.

Let me be clear: All positive recognition is a good thing. However, some ways of doing it tend to have greater impact for the individual and the organization than others.

As you read through the list, consider that the greatest value tends to come from recognition activity where the most people can see it and learn from it. Part of what makes the recognition "strategic" is that it becomes a way to share best practices that others will learn from and replicate.

High impact:
- Post a "story" on an internal social recognition platform (such as an example of an employee acting in a way that has a positive impact on coworkers, customers, or the organization).
- Share a recognition in the form of a "shout out" or "thank you" at regularly scheduled meetings. Make sure to share the specifics of what the person did and why it was important.
- Write a personal (handwritten) note and either hand it to the person or, better yet, mail it to their home.
- Conduct in-person conversations, thanking the employee for doing their job well, going above and beyond, or creating a "wow" experience (more to come on these different types).
- Give a gift accompanied by a personal note. It does not have to be expensive—it's the thought that counts!

Lower impact (yet still important and often effective):
- Send an email to the individual or team.
- Send an e-card.
- Highlight a career milestone (in any of the above formats).
- Post a story to an external social media site (Facebook, Twitter, etc.).

First Downs, Touchdowns, and Championships

When the Dallas Cowboys (or any football team at any level) begin their season, they have one overarching goal: to win a championship. In the National Football League, the Super Bowl is the ultimate championship prize. People play offense, defense, or special teams and points can be scored by any of these groups. However, most of the points are scored by the offense, who are responsible for running plays that lead to first downs (which allow them to run more plays). After a number of plays, hopefully they've moved the ball down the field enough (achieving enough first downs) so they are in a position to either kick a field goal (three points) or score a touchdown (six points). I apologize to those of you who are not football fans, but I share this overly simplistic and incomplete overview because it will be helpful in determining WHAT to recognize people for doing.

So, in football, you achieve first downs that help position you for touchdowns, and if you get enough of those, you can win enough games to position yourself to play for and win the championship.

When you consider WHAT to recognize people for, it is helpful to think about these three objectives of a football team:

- First downs
- Touchdowns
- Championships

At work, there are a lot of **first downs** that happen day in and day out. First downs consist of the daily effort that people exert to drive success for themselves, their teams, and the organization. In some cases, a first down is nothing more than a person doing a really good job in their role—setting the standard. Recognizing these first downs helps them see they are on track, shows them you respect them, and helps them feel good about their effort and the impact they have.

Sometimes a first down is more of an above and beyond effort—something that goes beyond the standard job requirement. And in some cases, it leads to a best practice that can be shared so others can learn from it.

The highest-impact first downs are WOW moments—when an individual or a group of employees does something that has a big impact on the customer experience or heavily impacts one of the business result areas you most want to accelerate.

Whether a first down is a setting-the-standard, above-and-beyond, or a WOW moment doesn't matter as much as whether you successfully take the time to spot it and recognize it. It doesn't matter at this point whether a result has been achieved as long as the effort is there. Sometimes providing a little recognition that acknowledges the effort can be just what is needed to help inspire and motivate people to keep pressing on. Here are a few examples of effort level areas worthy of recognition:

- Helping out others
- Learning something new
- Sharing knowledge and expertise
- Providing great service to customers
- Solving a problem

How do you know when a first down is achieved? Four questions to ask yourself to determine if an effort level is worthy of recognition:

1. Was the effort aligned with the business results your organization is trying to accelerate? (You might not have achieved the result yet, but the effort is in alignment.)
2. Did the effort lead to a positive business result for your team or the organization?
3. Did the effort indirectly help someone else accelerate a business result or achieve a goal?
4. Was the effort intended to improve the work environment or customer experience?

First downs are critical to recognize as they are what fulfill the day-to-day cravings, keeping people motivated and committed to making touchdowns and winning championships.

Just like in football, you need first downs to score touchdowns. Sometimes you need lots of them. **Touchdowns** are key results that happen throughout the game. At work, touchdowns present a different opportunity for recognizing employees. With touch-downs, you are recognizing results that come about from effort level (first downs). This can be any type of outcome regardless of whether it is big or small, as long as it aligns with the organization's purpose, values, and/or the business results you are striving to accelerate. Results at work could include:

- A project success
- A goal achieved
- A team accomplishment
- A process improvement
- An innovative idea

Finally, we have **championships**. Obviously, they are nowhere near as frequent as effort level or key results, but when they happen it often pays to make a big deal about them. Championships to be recognized at work are major accomplishments and milestones that occur because of a lot of effort (first downs) and personal or team results (touchdowns) over time. Championships come in the shape of:

- Sales, revenue, or profitability goals
- Productivity or cost-saving goals
- Customer acquisition goals
- Career milestones
- Team milestones

WHAT TO RECOGNIZE PEOPLE FOR			
	FIRST DOWNS	**TOUCHDOWNS**	**CHAMPIONSHIPS**
WHAT TO LOOK FOR	effort level	key results	major accomplishments/milestones
TYPES	setting the standard above and beyond WOW moments	project/team success process improvement innovative idea	sales, productivity, or cost-saving goals career milestones team milestones

Three Steps to Being Strategic

Regardless of the type of recognition, make sure it is strategic, ensuring you fulfill the craving for respect and help the individual(s) get a sense of appreciation for the purpose of their work ... how they make a difference. This can be done by following the three simple steps below:

1. Tell the **ACTION**: Describe what the person did (behavior) that is worthy of being recognized. Be specific and do the recognition in a timely manner. Doing so shows the recognition recipient that you respect them for their effort and are helping them to see the purpose of their work.

> EXAMPLE: *Craig realized how chaotic our work area had become. We're so busy and sometimes forget to put tools back in the right place. Craig noticed we spent too much time looking for tools needed to keep the machines running optimally. He facilitated a new arrangement for storing our tools after each shift is over.*

2. **CONNECT** to a focus area: A focus area may be living the core values, performing a customer service experience, or implementing an "operational excellence" improvement program or any other behavior-based program. All require certain behaviors to be successful. It is important to link the action because doing so makes it clear that what the person did "makes a difference" in achieving a priority or goal for the organization. For this example, let's assume that one of the core values for this organization is "Be Operationally Efficient."

> **EXAMPLE:** *Craig's efforts are a great example of helping us live our value of being operationally efficient.*

3. Share the **IMPACT**: Note why it is important. In this step, it is critical to show the benefit of the action for the team, customers, or the organization as a whole. By sharing the impact, you are providing another healthy dose of respect and purpose!

> **EXAMPLE:** *The improved storage area has cut down on the time it takes us to adjust and fix our equipment. It also helps lengthen the uptime of our machines, which has improved our hourly production rate.*

Being a Trusted Leader Is a Balancing Act

Being strategic with your employee recognition makes you a better leader. And it's worth repeating ... this is absolutely not an exercise in manipulation! It's being strategic. You can only be accused of being manipulative if you are not genuine in your praise and only recognize for actions people demonstrate that help you reach your individual goals. By keeping the focus on the organization—its purpose, mission, values, and goals—as well as department or team goals, you will not come across as a self-serving leader. Instead, you will be viewed as a strategic, thoughtful, and trusted leader.

Are You a Trusted Leader?

Do employees who work with you trust you as much as you hope? If they don't, might strategic recognition be the perfect vehicle to help you build trust?

A few years ago, I was gearing up to take the stage at a company event on leadership. The opening act was Marshall Goldsmith, world-renowned business educator and coach. Goldsmith claimed his area of expertise to be helping successful people change behaviors, which he warned the audience was going to come across as incredibly easy to do, but also incredibly difficult to do. Goldsmith shared, "The more successful we get, two things happen: It becomes harder to get people to tell you the truth, and the better we feel about ourselves, the harder it becomes to hear the truth."[57] I found this perspective interesting as it relates to the self-perception I've found many leaders have regarding whether they do a solid, genuine, and strategic job recognizing employees. Goldsmith concluded from his own research that 98 percent of leaders see themselves in the top 50 percent of the most successful leaders in their firm.[58] This statistic is both surprising and entertaining. How could it be? I had to find out for myself.

98% of leaders believe they are in the top 50% of the most trusted and effective leaders in their organization

A week later, I was in front of an audience of about one hundred leaders from a manufacturing organization in the Midwest. So, I decided to run my own little research study to validate Goldsmith's findings.

ME. Show of hands ... How many of you are in the top 50 percent of the most trusted and effective leaders within this organization?

AUDIENCE. [*Awkward pause, then hands begin to go up ... lots of hands*]

ME. It looks as though about 90 percent or more of you have your hands up.

AUDIENCE. [*Quickly start to reflect; laughing slightly and looking around*]

ME. So at least 90 percent of you are in the top 50 percent of the most effective and trusted leaders?

AUDIENCE. [*More laughter*]

I conducted this poll several times over the next few months and guess what? I got the same results. What happened with each audience is both statistically insane and psychologically real. We tend to assume we are better leaders than we are. As humans, our overconfidence is not uncommon. In fact, studies show that 90 percent of us believe we are above average drivers. Think about this for a moment. Are you an above average driver? I know I think I am!

What Does Trust Look Like at Work?

I decided to expand my research efforts to better understand what people thought of when they heard the word "trust" in connection with leaders. My thinking was that maybe people have widely different perspectives of what trusts looks like in the workplace. In the back of my mind, I was looking to better understand how trust is impacted when humans are recognized in ways that help them get what they CRAVE. Could it be possible that strategically recognizing employees not only helps people feel respected and understand their purpose, but also helps them develop stronger relationships with a boss simply due to an increase in trust?

Therefore, at each speech for the next two years, I conducted my own research poll about trust. I explained that trust is not something that is given to a leader; it must be earned through the way the leader acts and interacts.

I asked audience members to think about a leader who earned their trust. Then I asked them to jot down a response to the following: "What is it they do that makes you trust them?"

I collected the responses and organized them into categories I dubbed attributes of a trusted leader. Over time, fifteen different attributes were in my notebook. What I discovered next was interesting. It appeared that being a trusted leader involved quite the balancing act between being both performance-focused (results, accountability, etc.) and focused on the human side of work.

The following table recaps the top themes I learned regarding what leaders most often do to earn trust.

ATTRIBUTES OF A TRUSTED LEADER	
Performance	**Humanity**
• Set clear direction & goals	• Be even-keeled: balanced & consistent
• Implement successfully	• Ask good questions
• Make decisions	• Actively listen
• Be assertive; not pushy or aggressive	• Help solve problems
• Be competent	• Take an interest in people's lives
• Take charge	• Protect people ("I got your back")
• Effectively communicate results	• Make time for one-on-ones
	• Focus on small wins
	• Give credit to others

What I continued to learn from my collaborations with audience members was that leaders who are too focused on performance are not optimally trusted. They are most often seen as go-getters, driven by results. Yes, you can count on performance-driven leaders to get the job done, but at what cost? Sometimes these leaders are seen as backstabbers who are only out for their own self-interest, achieving success at the expense of their people.

On the other hand, leaders who focus too heavily on humanity can be counted on to build relationships, show compassion, and be there for their team, yet are also not as trusted as they could be. Often, these leaders are seen as incompetent because they're not willing or able to hold others accountable for results. However, the attributes shared for this group clearly show they understand that success is achieved with people, not at the expense of people.

Success is achieved with people, not at the expense of people.

The saying "life is a balancing act" rings true for being an effective and trusted leader the same as it does for any other area of your life. Trust is earned, not awarded. So, are you as much of a trusted leader as you could be? Are you one of the 90 percent who think they are a trusted leader? Or are you one of the 50 percent who actually are?

Now, back to the role of the Ultimate Habit of strategically recognizing employees as a way to not only increase the trust you earn, but also help you balance both performance and humanity. Consider the logic: If you spot an example of someone demonstrating an effort that aligns with your organization's priorities and goals and you recognize them for it, are you not being both humanistic and focusing on performance? Of course you are. Especially when you follow the three steps to a strategic recognition. What makes it strategic goes beyond simply the focus on business results; it also positions you to earn more trust as a leader.

To recap: When you invest ten minutes a week to spot an example of a recognizable moment, you position yourself to be a more effective and trusted leader who balances both performance and humanity, while giving people more of what they CRAVE—sparking the release of brain chemicals that make people feel good and encourage them to do more of what you want them to do. And when you deliver recognition in a timely, concise way with the three steps of ACTION, CONNECT, and IMPACT, you will also get what you CRAVE: respect, purpose, and stronger relationships with your team. All while accelerating business results.

ACCELERATE THE CUSTOMER EXPERIENCE

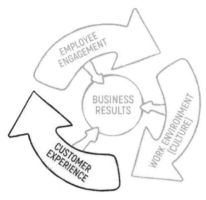

What is the goal of your organization? When I ask this question, what is the first thing that comes to mind? From my experience, many people's first reaction is "to make money." While this is absolutely an objective, it is not the primary goal. The one goal all organizations must achieve (in order to make more money) is to get and keep more profitable customers.

I didn't invent this idea. It's an offshoot of the definition coined by Peter Drucker, Harvard business professor and management guru, back in the 1980s when he said that for all companies to fulfill their purpose, they must create a customer.

A goal of every organization is to get and keep more profitable customers.

More than thirty years later, the purpose of a company remains the same: create customers. Yet a challenge many companies face is they spend so much time trying to get new customers that they lose focus on the tremendous efficiencies that can be created by delivering a better experience to existing ones. Better experiences rarely happen without a more engaged workforce, operating in a work environment that not only supports but drives the customer experience. In addition, you can create a new customer and do so unprofitably. Therefore, the goal today must include the element of serving and delivering the product/solution profitably.

Customers Deserve Engaged Employees

And if they don't get it from your organization, they will get it from a competitor. Or at least they will try to. My good friend Shep Hyken, best-selling author on the topic of the customer service experience, has a perspective that is difficult to refute: "Every statistic and fact out there indicates that service gives any company a competitive advantage, and the lack of it can be the demise of a business."[59]

With so many service channels available for customers (phone, email, chat, social media), it is easier than ever for them to make a switch. And switching they will do.

Businesses lose $62 billion per year through poor customer service. Even more shocking is that this number has increased by nearly 50 percent in the last three years.[60] Sixty-two billion dollars is a paltry number when compared to Accenture's report that in the past year, consumers switching providers because of poor service is estimated to cost businesses $1.6 trillion.[61] From my perspective, it doesn't really matter whether we are talking billions or trillions; something different needs to happen to help organizations improve the customer experience.

In a research study by New Voice Media, consumers were asked whether they have ever switched to a different business as a result of a bad customer service experience. The results? Forty-nine percent of respondents reported switching. And of those, 67 percent switched more than once. The main reasons were that the customers felt unappreciated, encountered unhelpful or rude staff, were redirected to multiple agents, were not able to speak to a person on the phone, were not able to get answers, or were put on hold for too long.[62]

As Hyken puts it, "It's not hard to figure out the implications of this. If you don't provide a good customer service experience, someone else out there is going to gain half of your existing customers."[63]

There are so many (huge understatement) research studies on the realities of good and bad customer experiences. Endless statistics heighten awareness that more focus and energy should be allocated to help customers feel better about their experience. Allow me to share with you one more statistic about the importance of providing strategic recognition in ways that help employees help customers "feel" better about their experience: Seventy percent of buying experiences are based on how the customer feels they are being treated.[64]

Stats like this are so simple to find. A quick Google search on "customer experience statistics" yielded 14,200,000 results in less than one second. More stats are not what we need. Well, maybe one more: Fifty-five percent of consumers say they would pay more for a better customer service experience.[65] Okay, that's it. That's all that's necessary to prove the need for more focus on what actually accelerates a better customer experience. You guessed it: more strategic employee recognition that shares examples of good (or better yet, great) service in action.

"If you don't provide a good customer service experience, someone else out there is going to gain half of your existing customers." [66]

Recognize What You Want to See More Of

Kathryn's organization provides service via a call center to thousands of customers every week. A priority for Kathryn and her workforce was to improve their "first call resolution" (FCR), meaning they would be able to handle an issue to the customer's liking on the first phone call. FCR is a simple metric to track, but it can be a complicated one to make sense of as acceptable levels differ by industry and type of service provided. In this example, the call center was supporting a professional services business and Kathryn's organization had struggled—historically achieving below industry average levels of FCR. In fact, they were 15 percent lower than the national average for their industry. Obviously, they wanted to accelerate these results in the future. So, what did they do? They took on the strategy to increase recognition of call center employees, which they did by 140 percent, making it a point to spot examples of actions that led to better customer experiences and highlighting when they happened on a first call. This resulted in a 25 percent increase in FCR over the course of five years. Not surprising, in the last year alone, employee engagement scores went up 32 percent in the call center.

REMEMBER: If you want to see more of something, then recognize the actions that lead to it. If you want to accelerate the customer experience, then make it a goal each week to find one example of employees providing the desired customer experience.

If you want to see more of something, recognize the actions that lead to it.

ACCELERATE BUSINESS RESULTS

Back to the Results You Want Most

Earlier, you considered the business results you want to accelerate in your work area. Results that are affected by the attitudes and actions of employees. Results that could be accelerated if only more engaged employees demonstrated those attitudes and actions  even more consistently than they do today.

Now let's get into the monetization of those results.

Below is an exercise to help you gain perspective and appreciate the actions people take at work that accelerate your results. Consider this the WHAT to recognize people for. I recommend starting this exercise on your own, then take it to your team and do it as a group as a way to get buy-in for the power of recognition. There are three steps to this exercise. The final step, monetizing results, may require a little extra effort to gather data and make assumptions about expected impact. I assure you, doing so will be worth your effort as you will find the conversation enlightening in regard to the economic value to be created.

141

Step 1: Choose a Business Result

Build or review your existing list of business results you want to accelerate. Choose one to focus on accelerating through strategic recognition.

MANUFACTURING & DISTRIBUTION

- Fewer quality issues
- Increased productivity
- Better on-time delivery
- Fewer safety incidents
- Decreased insurance costs
- Increased employee retention
- Less lost time due to injury or illness

RETAIL & HOSPITALITY

- Improved customer retention
- Increased customer acquisition
- Fewer complaints
- Lower employee turnover
- Less employee absenteeism
- Improved satisfaction and loyalty

PROFESSIONAL SERVICES

- Increased average sale per client
- Greater client retention
- More referrals
- Increased cross-selling and up-selling
- Fewer quality issues
- Decreased employee absenteeism
- Less time to fill a job

HEALTH CARE

- Improved patient satisfaction
- Increased quantity of patients
- Fewer patient complaints
- Increased program participation
- Improved quality of care outcomes
- Decreased employee turnover/absenteeism
- Fewer safety issues/incident reports

Step 2: Determine the Actions

What are the simple, but important, actions your team and others take that directly or indirectly influence the business result you want to accelerate?

For example, let's say your business result is increased customer loyalty. The actions to recognize would include:

1. Initiate follow-up with customers to ensure they have what they need.
2. Take the time to recommend additional solutions that add value for customers.
3. Double-check customer orders to ensure accuracy.

Each action clearly leads to a better customer experience (or helps avoid a bad one), thus has the potential to enhance customer loyalty. Once you have the key action, you can then round out the story to be shared. Remember, in addition to the ACTION, the other two components of a strategic recognition include: CONNECT it to a focus area and share the expected IMPACT. Doing so provides the respect and understanding of purpose that people CRAVE.

Below I provide some examples of how to connect IMPACT to each of the actions in my previous example.

1. Following up with customers to make sure they have what they need helps instill confidence for the customer, which leads to repeat business and more referrals.

2. Recommending additional solutions that add value strengthens the customer relationship with our organization and increases sales.

3. Double-checking order accuracy decreases product returns or costly rework that affects profits and frustrates customers.

Step 3: Strive to Monetize Results with Real ROI

In this last step, you need to do a little work to gather financial numbers (or at least make some logical assumptions) to explore the true cost savings or revenue generation resulting from employees' actions. This step has proved to be a terrific group exercise to win over the hearts and minds of leaders, especially those who may be Recognition Results Doubters.

For each of our three examples above, I'll provide assumptions (for illustration purposes) that help monetize the business results:

1. Average customer sale is $1,000 with a profit margin of 30 percent. Customer buys one more time per year and provides one referral per year because of the increased confidence. Total revenue increase of $2,000 per customer. Profit = $600.

2. Average upsell based on employee recommendations is $100. Assume employee successfully upsells 10 percent of the time and handles a hundred customer calls per day. Upsell per employee is $1,000 per day. Not bad for a day's work.

3. Product returns cost $50 per order. There are typically ninety returns per day. Double-checking order accuracy eliminates 10 percent of mistakes, decreasing return costs by $450 a day.

Again, these figures are for illustration purposes to show you how, with a little bit of thought (and cost/sales figures), you can begin to run forecasts that will help leaders and employees more clearly see the impact of their work.

If you've made it this far … I assume you are a believer. As you jump into Part 3, you will learn how investing 10 Minutes by Friday to do the Ultimate Habit will accelerate the business results you want more of.

Part 3: Mastering the Ultimate Habit™

Strategic recognition is simple and easy to do.
Unfortunately, it's even easier not to do it.

In Part 1, we explored the decades of evidence about what helps people become more motivated at work. In Part 2, we looked at the Recognition Is the Accelerator Model and I shared some real-life examples of business results accelerated. It is my hope that you found everything to be simple to understand and yet insightful. In this part, we will dive into how to create and sustain the Ultimate Habit. But before we do, I want to address a potential challenge some of you may face.

This challenge especially applies to those of you who are already quite successful leaders ... or at least you perceive yourself as being successful. From my experience, successful people give themselves very few reasons to change their behavior and lots of reasons to stick with the status quo, that is, what they believe has helped make them successful. This belief in their success provides positive reinforcement, so they feel it's smart to continue doing what they've always done. We create some self-delusion, and it feels good.

Feeling good is something we'd all like more of. To what extent will our brains naturally take us there? According to Cordelia Fine, an academic psychologist and researcher who wrote three books on neuroscience and psychology, our brains will go to great lengths to help us feel good. Fine coined the term the "Vain Brain," a phenomenon she studied and documented in her best-selling book, *A Mind of Its Own*. According to Fine, "the brain can selectively edit and censor the truth, both about ourselves and the world, making for a softer, kinder, and altogether more palatable reality."[67] She explains how our Vain Brain excuses our faults, or simply ignores them. Our brains routinely lie to us and go to amazing lengths to bias our perceptions in our favor. As humans, we tend to take credit for successes and blame others for failures. Our brains have a way of helping us selectively edit our memories to preserve our self-image.

It would appear that the higher up we go in an organization the more successful we feel. Which isn't a bad thing—unless we start to believe a few too many of our own press clippings. The reality is at the higher levels of management, most of the leading players are quite smart and technically skilled. In most cases, that's why they got to where they are with the responsibilities of managing systems and humans. And this is exactly why the Ultimate Habit of strategically recognizing employees is even more important for those who've risen up the leadership ranks. Quite often, even greater responsibility is placed on top leaders to create the environment where employees feel respected and understand the relevance, meaning, and purpose of their work.

As you read Part 3, keep in mind, all things being equal, your habits (or lack thereof) are more noticeable the higher up you go. People are closely watching what you say and, more importantly, what you do. The expectation-setting, communication, and accountability behaviors you demonstrate often make the difference in how trusted and successful you are as a leader. In the pages that follow, I'll guide you through processes, stories, and suggestions to encourage you to disrupt business as usual and take on new ways of thinking and acting. I only ask that you keep an open mind, regardless of how simple some of the steps may seem, and demonstrate a willingness to try a few new routines that have proven to fuel the work environment with more of what people CRAVE!

With this perspective in mind, it's my opinion that every supervisor, manager, and executive—no matter what title, rank, level of busyness or responsibility—CAN become a more effective and trusted leader who creates an even better place to work, leading to better customer experiences. And you will accomplish this WHEN you invest up to ten minutes a week to stop, think about, and/or actively recognize employees in a way that connects their effort to the specific business results that matter most to your organization.

That's right: You have the power to give people what they CRAVE! The power to increase the meaning of work, reduce workplace stress, and increase employee engagement.

While there may be several effective ways to give people what they CRAVE … my hope is that by this point in the book you'll agree none are as simple to do, cost-effective, or powerful as investing a few minutes a week to strategically recognize employees. A few minutes by Friday … that's all it takes.

As previously covered, we continue to suffer from an engagement crisis (energy crisis) where the great majority of employees (two-thirds) are not as motivated and committed as leaders (and customers) would like. Regardless of how much money organizations continue to pump into employee engagement and culture improvement initiatives, the results are usually a far cry from the expectations wishful leaders have. However, this is not the case for workforces where leaders follow the Ultimate Habit process you are about to learn. Instead, these leaders achieve remarkable engagement levels with more than 90 percent of employees motivated and committed at work. These leaders do three things very well:

1. They change their mindset, getting more comfortable with considering new ways of thinking.
2. They adopt new behaviors and routines.
3. They pay attention to the positive impact over time, both personally and to their organization.

At the beginning, I shared my goal that every reader, by the end of this book, would be asking, "Why the heck aren't more people using the power of recognition?" Hopefully by now you are asking this question and are willing to take on the challenge of committing to 10 Minutes by Friday.

10 Minutes by Friday can help cure the engagement crisis.

We All Have 'Should Lists;' We Should Have 'Must' Lists

We all have lists (even if they only exist in our minds) of the stuff we need to do. When we have something on our "should" list, we may desire to do it, but if we don't, we tend to let ourselves off easy. "Oh well, I didn't get to it." But when something is on our "must" list, we put a bit more pressure on ourselves, taking ownership to get it done. Coming up, we will cover how to ensure the Ultimate Habit is on your must-do list every week.

I have to warn you—accomplishing any habit requires changing behaviors. And changing behaviors ... well ... it's not very easy to do. In fact, changing behavior is overwhelming for some, terrifying for others, and downright uncomfortable for just about everyone else. Consider New Year's resolutions. Research says close to 60 percent of people make resolutions, but only around 9 percent will actually achieve their goals.[68]

Changing behavior is overwhelming for some, terrifying for others, and downright uncomfortable for just about everyone else.

According to U.S. News & World Report, 80 percent of New Year's resolutions fail by the second week of February, which begs the question, "Why is it that with such good intentions, getting fit, losing weight and improving our lives seems so elusive?"[69]

As humans, we struggle so mightily to keep our behavior-change promises that we now have a holiday to poke fun at ourselves. That's right, a holiday! January 17 has recently been deemed "Ditch Your New Year's Resolution Day." The attitude shared by one popular online time and date site is:

> *You have done well for the past couple of weeks. You have stuck to your New Year's resolutions. But are now ready to give them up. You are busy, you took on too much, that piece of cake just looks [too] darn good to ignore. Whatever your reason to break your New Year resolutions, you can do it guilt-free on Ditch Your New Year's Resolution Day.[70]*

Not surprising, there is a clinical term for the cycle of repeated failed attempts to change our behavior and improve ourselves: False Hope Syndrome. One study sought to uncover why people repeatedly attempted to make self-change happen despite continuous failures. The author reported that when people do actually change (which is not common), they feel great. However, even when unsuccessful, people still feel some initial reward: "Feelings of control and optimism often accompany the early stages of self-modification efforts."[71]

Please consider: What are the chances you would change long-standing behaviors (diet, lack of exercise, smoking, etc.) if you were in a life-or-death situation? Probably 100 percent, right? Not a chance you'd ever ignore or completely disregard anything as important as staying alive!

What if you had heart bypass or angioplasty surgery and your doctor provided astounding evidence that you must make changes to your diet and exercise habits or you will die? Will you change? Well, research shows that the great majority of people don't. According to Dr. Edward Miller, former CEO of Johns Hopkins University Medical School:

> *If you look at people after coronary-artery bypass grafting two years later, 90% of them have not changed their lifestyle. And that's been studied over and over and over again. And so we're missing some link in there. Even though they know they have a very bad disease and they know they should change their lifestyle, for whatever reason, they can't.*[72]

This is incredible. Only about 10 percent of people make the changes necessary after heart surgery! Even when presented with overwhelming evidence that we should change the way we act and do something different, something better for us and for our loved ones, we don't. Even when NOT changing could cause us to DIE we still struggle to change our behavior.

Bottom line? Changing a behavior is hard! One might argue that asking an adult to change their behavior is one of the most difficult things you can ask them to do. WHY is this? The reasons are usually not because people are bad or stupid. Instead, the usual cause is a lack of understanding on HOW to change. In fact, I would suggest that most people know more about how to fix their cars than they do about how to make a positive behavior change stick. And let's face it: Most of us don't have any clue how to fix our cars when something goes wrong.

What Was the Most Memorable Behavior Change You've Made Recently?

Remember that question I asked you in the Introduction, the one I asked you to let simmer? What significant or memorable behavior change have you recently made in your life? What comes to mind? If you are like most, you thought of behaviors you've tried to change. Behaviors you wish you had changed—for example, eating healthier, exercising more, being more organized at work, thinking positively, spending more time with your kids, being a nicer person, meditating—the list can go on and on.

The reason for the constant failure to change behaviors is that we don't know how to create and sustain habits.

That all changes now! Let's dive into the world of habits, what they are, how to make them stick, and how to apply the habit-building process to make strategic recognition the Ultimate Habit for fueling what humans CRAVE at work.

Since changing the way we act is hard, it requires a little bit of structure: the right mindset, specific behaviors, some willpower, and a belief that the change is going to be beneficial. As you will learn, these make up key components of a habit.

Thus far we've thoroughly explored the idea that if you provide employees more of what they CRAVE (by recognizing them more often for their effort and results), they will be more motivated and committed (engaged) at work, driving measurable and monetizable increases in engagement, productivity, and customer growth. However, before we jump into the process for creating the Ultimate Habit, allow me to share some background information on habits. You may find this beneficial since the habit-building process is applicable to any positive habit you want to create in your life.

We fail to change behavior because we don't know how to create and sustain habits.

Humans, By Nature, Are Creatures of Habit

What the heck is a habit? A habit is a thought or action that is repeated over and over until it becomes automatic and almost effortless. Humans are creatures of habit. Each day we are directed by hundreds of habits. It's simply part of being human. Scientists and researchers have been studying human behavior and reporting facts about habits for decades. Would it surprise you to know that 95 percent of our thoughts and 45 percent of our behaviors are habitual?[73] [74] That's right: Most of what we think about and almost half of our daily actions are done because that's the way we've always done them! How we think influences how we behave, which makes up the habits that define our character.

So, when it comes to considering your habits, consider this …

You can either create and reinforce habits that bring positive outcomes or continue with habits that bring challenges and lost opportunities.

Think of a habit as a choice you intentionally make at some point in time. Initially, when you make this choice, extreme focus and energy are needed. Eventually it becomes natural for you to continue doing it over and over because it feels good. Because there is some recognizable benefit of doing the action.

You Brush Your Teeth Every Day, Don't You?

Of course you do. Because if you didn't, you would feel gross. You'd have a bad taste in your mouth. And your breath wouldn't help you win any new friends or keep existing ones. But think for a moment: How unnatural would brushing your teeth be for an early human? Imagine a caveman living in prehistoric times with a family of Neanderthals. His friend walks into the cave with a weird object in hand. It's a small brush at the end of a short stick. On it is an interesting, sticky, soft paste. The friend suggests the caveman put the brush in his mouth and swirl it around. How unnatural might this have been for him? At first, maybe he'd think, "This is crazy, why would I do this?" But his friend would insist, "You've got to try this." So he does. It's a bit uncomfortable. He brushes. He spits. He brushes some more. Spits it out. He agrees to keep trying this each morning. After a few days, he begins to appreciate the fresh taste in his mouth. Then he realizes that some of the caveladies are taking notice. They seem to want to be around him more. They even begin to volunteer to help gather firewood. Life is great ... so he continues to brush, often doing so a few times a day. Before he knows it, brushing his teeth is a daily habit ... just like it is for you and me. Every day we brush our teeth without any conscious thought. Why? Because it's habitual.

The same can be said for taking a shower. Showering isn't an instinctive habit. I have three kids. Getting them to shower when they were little wasn't always easy. As they grow, it becomes habitual. Why? Because they see the consequences when they don't. Not showering means you SMELL BAD! You look grimy. Others think poorly of you! Your mindset about showering changes and so do your routines—you begin to shower more often.

Think about other areas of your life beyond personal hygiene. Are you interested in living a healthier life? Consider habits around exercising, eating healthier, sleeping more, or taking time for personal reflection each day. Consider financial habits. Should you be saving more, sharing more? What about habits that improve your relationships? Are there people you know you should spend more time with? Are there things you could be doing to be more approachable or friendlier? That's right, you can create habits that will help you be a nicer person.

There are many habits you could be working on to improve yourself as a human, and the process we are embarking on will serve as a terrific guide. Personally, I've used it for a variety of behavior modification improvements for myself as well as other leaders I've coached who want to become healthier, better humans at work. When you are done with this book, I encourage you to apply the habit-building process to other areas of your life where more consistent behaviors and routines will enhance your well-being at home and at work.

A Habit Is a Gift

A habit is a gift we've all been given. It's an amazing achievement tool that will perform the actions you've programmed it to perform without conscious thought. But to receive this gift, you have to follow a process. I realize some people have contempt for structure and may struggle to follow something that is too prescribed. But, from my experience, we tend to not get much better in changing our behaviors without a little structure. Stick with me to create the Ultimate Habit of strategically recognizing employees and establishing the ongoing accountability to sustain your habit over time.

FIVE STEPS TO CREATING A HABIT.
SIMPLE AND EASY!

There are five steps to making a habit stick. Trust me when I tell you that you don't want to skip any of the five steps. If you do, I can assure you there will be predictable consequences ... you will struggle to make the habit stick. So why take the chance? Plan to complete each step.

Before we begin, I have good news and bad news. Good news first: You will find this process to be simple and easy to do. But the bad news shouldn't be ignored: Unfortunately, at the same time, it will be even easier not to do it. Consider this possibility: Most of you are already *not* doing employee recognition or at least not doing it as strategically as you could. You may have excuses (which we will address). You may be unaware of the powerful benefits (which we will also address). You may think you are already maximizing effectiveness with a current approach or program (which you are probably not) or you may simply be a jerk who doesn't like people (which I'm going to assume you are not, as jerks would never get this far in a book about giving people what they CRAVE). In the case of having excuses, being unaware of the powerful benefits, or coziness with your current approach, it may be easier to continue on the path of least resistance. Don't let this happen. Disrupt business as usual. Try something new. What do you have to lose? Especially since the Ultimate Habit can be performed amazingly well in as little as ten minutes a week.

10 Minutes by Friday™: The Ultimate Habit™ Challenge

Imagine investing ten minutes every week to do an activity that gives you the power to make others around you better. An activity that fuels the work environment with the respect and appreciation that others CRAVE. An activity that literally makes you a more effective and trusted leader.

Leaders who do a great job recognizing employees commit to a small investment of time each week.

10 Minutes by Friday!

That's it! Ten minutes each week to be strategic in recognizing employees. I'm not suggesting that you must write a strategic recognition every single week. The goal is to take the time to think about an effort or result worthy of recognition. A ten-minute investment very often leads to recognitions that truly accelerate engagement and improvements in the customer experience. In addition, it's an investment you make that begins to positively impact the business outcomes you want most.

And let's be honest here. It's such a small amount of time that has a very big payback. Let's explore for a moment just how little this time investment really is. If we do some math on this ten-minute investment of time, it adds up to a few hours a year.

Think about it. If you commit to the goal of 10 Minutes by Friday, you will share a strategic recognition some weeks and some weeks you won't because you may not witness anything worthy of sharing. But at the end of the month, if you've demonstrated your habit at least a few times, you will be doing a very good job. You don't need to be perfect. You do need to make progress in making employee recognition strategic, genuine, and results-focused. And if you are able to find and share a success every week, you will be doing an amazing job!

So ... we can diffuse the "time bomb" right now. It's simply NOT a rational excuse because EVERYONE has at least ten minutes a week they could invest to consider an opportunity to recognize an employee in a way that fulfills their craving. Especially if it accelerates motivation, engagement and stronger performance.

To help guide you through the five steps to creating the Ultimate Habit, download the worksheet from www.gregglederman.com/ultimatehabit. Really, put down this book for a few minutes and visit the site to download the worksheet. That way you can complete the Ultimate Habit as you read through the best practices that make it simple and easy.

Let's get started with Step 1.

STEP 1: DECIDE ON A MINDSET

The first step in making strategic recognition a habit is to decide on a mindset. Building any habit requires behavior change, and behavior change requires a change in thinking, a "rewiring of the brain" that takes a little time and persistence. Once your mindset is in place, it will shape your attitude and influence the very behaviors you need to power the habit. The mindset you

begin with helps strengthen your reasons for strategically recognizing employees. Many managers say they are committed to recognizing effectively, but their <u>reasons</u> are simply not strong enough. In those cases, they are at risk of their <u>excuses</u> taking over.

What do you need to change your mind about to keep the habit of recognizing employees a high priority?

The most often-cited mindset I hear time and again from leaders who have gone on to be super successful at making recognition an accelerator of their success is:

It's simple to do and only takes a few minutes.

If you can commit to the goal of 10 Minutes by Friday, then this mindset is extra important.

Another popular mindset is:

It's important to recognize people for doing their job and doing it well.

All too often, leaders mistakenly think an employee has to go way above and beyond, demonstrating a WOW moment, if they are to be recognized. This faulty thinking can lead to lost opportunities to acknowledge when someone sets the standard for their role by giving the effort that qualifies as doing a "good job." What if you have an employee who typically falls short in doing a part of their job, but then all of a sudden, they do it pretty well? Doesn't it make sense to share a little appreciation for that effort? Of course it does! As stated earlier, if you want to see more of something, then recognize those actions when you see them. And keep in mind, it takes a lot of first downs and touchdowns to win the championship.

Here is one more example of a mindset to consider:

Effectively recognizing employees is a great way to share best practices and create learning moments.

With this mindset, you are paying homage to the fact that not only does recognition help the individual perform better, but it also enables you to share best practice examples that help others in the organization replicate the ideal attitudes, behaviors, and experiences. Now that is being strategic!

Take a moment to consider any additional mindsets you feel will be important in shaping your thinking to ensure you keep your commitment to making employee recognition a habit.

STEP 2: CREATE ROUTINES AND BEHAVIORS

If you are to keep your commitment to recognizing employees with a time investment of 10 Minutes by Friday, you will surely need a few routines to guide you. But, let's not complicate this step. There are three very specific routines that are highly recommended by those who do employee recognition very well. As a matter of fact, I've heard from managers at all levels that following these routines changed their lives at work, helping them to communicate more effectively with their teams and inspire higher performance.

First routine: *Schedule it.*

Put time for recognizing and sharing success on your calendar as a weekly appointment. What gets scheduled tends to get done. And, if you add it to Friday morning, then it's there all week on your calendar as a constant reminder of your commitment to (at a minimum) think about potential recognizable employee efforts or results achieved. I recommend setting the appointment for earlier in the day so there's less of a chance you will put it

169

off because other things come up or you get too stressed
and tired.

Dawn DePerrior, CIO of Constellation Brands, says, "Scheduling a few minutes each week helps me stay focused on finding
examples of the good things our people are doing to bring our
values to life. It makes it easy to keep the power of recognition
top of mind each week."

Second routine: *Conduct the One-Minute Reminder.*

This is a simple routine. Add one minute to the front end of the
agenda for a regularly scheduled meeting. During that sixty seconds, highlight an example of someone doing something that
helped make for a better place to work, enhanced productivity,
or enabled a good, if not great, customer experience. Consider
any first downs, touchdowns, or championships that others
should know about. You can also ask others on your team if they
have any examples of recognition to share with the group.

This sharing of appreciation and best practices not only fuels the
work environment with the recognition people CRAVE, it can
also change the tone of your meetings to be more positive and
productive. And you may find that your team will love it, as
Doug, a key leader in a large hospital, found out when he accidentally forgot to conduct the One-Minute Reminder at his
weekly team meeting. Doug wasn't so sure how the One-Minute

Reminder would be perceived at these meetings. He shared with me that he felt it would be a little "hokey," but was willing to give it a try. For the next three weeks, he began each meeting asking if someone had a "living the values moment" to share. And each week, team members shared a few examples. In the fourth week, they had a packed schedule and Doug accidentally forgot to open up with the One-Minute Reminder. As they were about to close the meeting, one of his teammates spoke up: "Wait, we haven't shared a 'living the values moment.'" Doug told me that he thought there was going to be a revolt, as others piped up suggesting they shouldn't end the meeting without taking the sixty seconds to quickly acknowledge a success. Doug admitted that he never expected his team would care so much.

The idea of a One-Minute Reminder is often used in the form of "safety moments" by organizations in the manufacturing and distribution industries. In these settings, safety is a non-negotiable core value that, if broken, can lead to serious injury if not death. Therefore, safety is always a priority and it becomes habitual for management to talk about it daily. While the Ultimate Habit does not combat life and death situations, there's no reason not to treat it with a routine that you know will keep it top of mind for managers to perform. In addition, sharing successes at team gatherings reinforces the key strategic areas of your business you want to accelerate. You'll find conducting One-Minute Reminders is a great way to highlight how employee actions link to your organization's core values, service standards, and safety moments, or simply reinforce any high-priority behavior-based initiative.

Third Routine: *Link to an existing weekly habit.*

You may have weekly habits already established, such as submitting expense reports, posting a schedule, or completing a progress report. If this is the case, you've already built a routine. Why not commit to achieving your 10 Minutes by Friday goal as part of that weekly activity? Stop, ask yourself if you witnessed something worthy of employee recognition in the past few days, and, if so, take the initiative to strategically recognize that employee either before or after you complete your already established task.

Before we move on to Step 3, take a moment to think of any other routines or behaviors you feel will help you master the Ultimate Habit.

STEP 3: DEMONSTRATE WILLPOWER

As I said earlier, the good news is the Ultimate Habit is simple and easy to do. Nothing we've covered so far is very difficult in theory or task. However, the bad news when it comes to making your habit stick is that, in most cases, it will be even *easier* to not do it. As a leader, you've been participating in meetings for years, and you've done so without taking the extra step to do a quick round of applause or shout out to appreciate and recognize someone's efforts. You've been scheduling your week ahead for as long as you can remember, but you've never scheduled a task to strategically recognize a success and share it so the employee feels appreciated and so that others can learn from it. This doesn't make you a bad person or bad leader. It's just not something that you've prioritized as super important and put the routine of a weekly appointment on your calendar to do. So naturally, *not* doing it is even easier. You won't need to change anything.

Making a new habit requires a little extra thought and energy to get it going. And part of this extra energy and thought requires you to plan for the inevitable willpower obstacles.

Before I get into what I mean by willpower obstacles, I want to forewarn you. This is the very step that most people are tempted to skip. DON'T! Skipping this step leads to predictable consequences. Ignoring the willpower obstacles will make it very difficult to keep the consistency going with your chosen routines and behaviors.

Willpower is the ability to do what really matters, even when at times it might seem difficult. Running out of willpower can ruin your habit.

Willpower is interesting. As it turns out, our willpower is in short supply each day and deteriorates when we get stressed and tired. So, with the design of any habit, you must predict where and when you might run out of willpower. Where might you be tempted to forget or simply decide not to do it? Predicting where you may fail is not an act of being negative. You are actually taking initiative to be self-compassionate, which will increase your chances of success over time.

Below are a few potential obstacles that can block your strategic recognition habit, along with a few ideas you can do to avoid them. As you read these, if you think of others, jot them down on your worksheet. You'll want to know what they are so you can go back to Steps 1 and 2 to make sure you have the right mindset and routines in place to help you avoid the obstacles and keep your willpower at a high level.

So, what do you think is the most common obstacle people cite?

You are not going to find this to be very surprising, but I think you'll agree it's completely irrational.

Are you ready? The number one willpower obstacle I hear over and over is:

"I'm so busy ... I don't have time."

This is the big one! The great big obstacle that is actually quite easy to solve. Why? Because if you are super busy, then you can't afford to not make strategically recognizing employees a great big priority each week.

Remember Jeff from the nursing home? He challenged his leaders to commit to ten minutes each week to stop, think about, and share an example of their core values in action linked to a business result. His fifty managers led the way (many doing it every week) to more than seven thousand shared stories in two years, which helped increase employee engagement by 125 percent, drive down employee turnover by 14 percent, and increase customer satisfaction by 20 percent. All of these accelerated results led to tremendous time savings in the form of fewer headaches, greater productivity, and less need to recruit, train, and develop new employees.

Consider this with respect to your organization and the business results you want to accelerate. The more you strategically recognize people, the more you get people to think about and do things the way you want them done. This lowers your stress, lessens your workload, and, yes, saves you time! If more people are doing what you want them to do, if more employees are engaged at work, if your work culture is improving, if productivity is higher, if turnover goes down, if the customer experience is also improving, then won't this save you time like it did for Jeff and his team of leaders? Of course it will! Now who doesn't have time for that?

If you are busy, then you can't afford to not make strategically recognizing employees a great big priority each week.

You do have the time. Take 10 Minutes by Friday to stop and think about whether you've witnessed something worthy of employee recognition and you're doing a great job! And consider this: If you do this every week, maybe some weeks you do a recognition and some weeks you can't come up with one. Let's assume you have a 50 percent success rate of actually thinking about and doing a strategic recognition. That means you're spending about twenty minutes of your time each month—at the most—and about three to six hours of your time over the course of a year. That's it ... about a half-day of work for most people to do something that improves employee engagement, leading to better customer experiences and better business results. Again, who doesn't have time for that!?

Here is another common example of a willpower obstacle:

"I didn't see any examples of success this week."

Often this obstacle presents itself when a leader doesn't have visibility into the daily actions of employees, or sometimes it's a result of a workforce that is spread out across many locations—especially a virtual workforce with many people working from home offices.

Either way, an easy solution is to add to your list of routines (in Step 2) the task of speaking with another employee, business partner, or maybe even a customer and asking them how things are going. Quite often, this effort, coupled with a little "investigation" and a few probing questions, can lead to a terrific opportunity to learn about the good, if not great, actions of others, the type of activity that is worthy of a little praise.

For instance, I am frequently on the road and don't get to see firsthand the work that is done with clients. But I do get the opportunity to chat with client leaders on a regular basis. So, I simply ask them, "How are things going?" and inevitably I learn about how a teammate has delivered the Brand Integrity Experience (our core values). All it takes is a few follow-up questions

177

with the client and I learn the very specific actions that I can strategically recognize someone for—and that others can learn from!

A third willpower obstacle I hear quite often is:

"My boss doesn't recognize me."

For years, managers have shared this willpower obstacle with me. It's as real as it is unfortunate, especially for frontline supervisors and managers who are fighting the fights each day to drive productivity, take care of customers, and achieve results. At Brand Integrity, we've learned something eye-opening regarding leaders who have a boss who either doesn't understand the power of employee recognition or simply is unwilling to share praise. What we've learned is that if you take the time to recognize these leaders (your boss), they are more apt to begin recognizing others, including you. At first, I didn't believe it. But sure enough, we ran an analysis using the data from across all clients in Brand Integrity's social recognition platform and it turns out there is an extremely high correlation ($r = 0.7$) showing that when leaders don't recognize others, but then get recognized, they in return begin posting recognitions. That's right. They actually experience the benefits, getting what they CRAVE. They then feel respected and have a greater understanding of the importance of the work they do, and sure enough they begin to recognize others more actively. Therefore, if one of your willpower obstacles is that your boss isn't a believer, and in fact is a Recognition Results Doubter, then go ahead and recognize them a few times in the coming months and watch what happens. I realize this may be uncomfortable for some people, but give it a try!

These three willpower obstacles probably cover the great majority of challenges that prevent people from achieving their goal of 10 Minutes by Friday. Might you have a few other willpower obstacles that will get in your way? If so, jot them down and make sure you have the ideal mindset and routines in place to overcome them.

STEP 4: FOCUS ON BENEFITS

Researchers and scientists who make a living studying human behavior tell us that around 77 percent of people maintain focus on a goal for a week or less and then slip back into old routines and habits.[75]

All too often, when we don't see a positive change right away, we struggle to keep the commitment we make to ourselves. In this case, you may end up with a few too many <u>excuses</u> for why you can't keep your commitment to proactively recognizing employee successes.

Let's not let that happen! In this step, you have the chance to double up the <u>reasons</u> WHY you are committed to strategically recognizing successes at work. These reasons will overpower any excuses that could diminish your willpower.

To get started, ask yourself these two questions: First, how will demonstrating the Ultimate Habit of strategically recognizing employees make a positive difference in your life? Second, how might it make a positive difference in the acceleration of the business results you want? Think back to the business results you thought about earlier in this book.

Any benefits that come out of this step coupled with your mind-set from Step 1 will help you drive your reasons why through the roof, while helping you to minimize excuses that can block your success.

Over time, focusing on the benefits will help you sustain your energy, your will, and your commitment to being successful.

Let's go over some ideas to get you started.

I've done the Ultimate Habit process with thousands of leaders. Here are the most common personal and business benefits I hear most frequently. Make note of those that are most meaningful to you.

First, some Personal Benefits:
- "I feel like a better leader. (Because I understand more clearly the positive impact I have on our culture.)"
- "I feel less stress at work."
- "More people understand expectations and do things the way we need them done."
- "I have a greater sense of pride in making progress on something that was not natural, or not easy, for me to do."

Now for some common Business Benefits to consider:
- Increased employee engagement and productivity
- Less employee turnover

- Lowered operational costs
- Happier customers who have a more consistent experience
- Improved quality
- More employees focused on the highest-priority goals and objectives

As you complete the Focus on Benefits step, keep in mind that you must be forward-thinking. Imagine what success will look like and feel like when you make the effort to recognize employees on a more regular basis. Can you think of any other benefits that you could add to the list?

STEP 5: TRACK EFFORT DAILY

Now we've arrived at the fifth and final step. Congratulations on getting this far. You are almost there! You can't stop now though. The fifth and final step will guarantee your success. That's right, I just said GUARANTEE. We all know there are very few guarantees in life. Ben Franklin famously gave us two things he said were certain in life: death and taxes. Well I am about to give you a third certainty, a true guarantee that you will make progress on performing the Ultimate Habit.

But to get the guarantee, you need to do a tiny bit of work.

Take a few seconds each workday to ask yourself, "Did I TRY to see someone doing something that was a recognizable moment? Did I TRY to spot a success at work?"

Take notice: You are not asking yourself whether you actually recognized someone. You're asking whether you even tried to spot a recognizable moment—a little extra effort, someone going above and beyond, or maybe even a WOW experience. If you do this for five seconds a day, I GUARANTEE you will improve! I can guarantee that you will make positive progress and get better than you are today at strategically recognizing employees, leading to at least some of the benefits you've been thinking about.

That's it, only a few seconds each workday to rewire your brain, reinforcing that your desired habit is a high priority. The reality is, what we track determines where we focus and what we are motivated to improve. Daily tracking, for as little as a few seconds a day, will ensure you take the time to reflect on your mindset, routines, and behaviors. And I guarantee, if you do it, you will make progress. You will get better.

This idea of daily tracking is not a new concept. In fact, it was Ben Franklin, more than 250 years ago, who mastered daily tracking to accomplish tremendous success in life. One could easily make the case that Ben Franklin is the most accomplished human ever! Here are a few of his accomplishments:

- One of the founding fathers of America
- Mapped the Gulf Stream
- Created bifocal glasses and the Franklin stove
- Invented the flexible catheter (thank you very little)
- Spearheaded and greatly influenced many staples we take for granted today, including the first library for lending books, the first public hospital, and the first university back in 1749

These are a few of his many accomplishments in a lifetime packed with tremendous, innovative successes. How did he do all of this?

Late in his life, Franklin wrote his autobiography and attributed his ability to set and track daily thoughts and behaviors as his secret to success. That's right; he attributed his lifetime of successes to his daily effort to track as a method for self-improvement.

Here is what Ben Franklin did: He created thirteen virtues to guide how he would think and act. Each of his virtues was in essence a habit that guided a series of thoughts and behaviors he felt were important. His virtues included things like: be sincere, demonstrate justice, have high resolve, demonstrate moderation, and be humble.

According to his autobiography, he developed these habits by focusing on one virtue each week. And each day of the week, he tracked the virtue as to whether he "lived it," asking himself, "Did I do it?" At the end of the week, he would review how many days he felt he demonstrated the virtue. Then he would pick another virtue for the next week. He would cycle through each virtue four times during the year.

Now Ben Franklin, for all his successes that have benefited our world, was not perfect. Far from it. In fact, while one of his virtues was chastity, he was known to be quite the philanderer. He wrote about his extramarital affairs in his memoir. Like all of us, he was a work in progress. Ben Franklin understood the key ingredient to successfully mastering habits: Progress, not perfection! He did most of his virtues, most of the time.

Want another example? Maybe Ben Franklin from the mid- to late 1700s is simply too far back.

Can becoming funny be a habit? Jerry Seinfeld thinks so. In my opinion, Seinfeld could be regarded as one of the funniest humans ever. When asked by a reporter how he became so funny, he shared his daily tracking approach to creating the habit of writing humorous material. His approach is called "Don't Break the Chain."

I'm paraphrasing what Seinfeld said in response to being asked how he became so funny. He said that before he became famous for his TV show, he was just trying to survive by doing standup comedy at local clubs. He had a strong desire to become funnier. So, he began to force himself to write down something funny each and every day. He purchased a large desk calendar and each month would tape it up on his bedroom wall. Then, each day he would try to write down one thing he saw or thought of that he thought was funny. Over time, he made thinking about and writing down funny ideas a habit. And collected a ton of material in the process.

So, what do these examples mean to you? Well, for one, you are not trying to become one of the most accomplished humans ever or the funniest person in the world, or the greatest leader on Planet Earth. You are simply trying to master one habit—the habit of strategically recognizing employees. And tracking your effort each workday by taking a few seconds to consider your effort ("Did I try?") will guarantee your success.

And tracking has never been easier.

There Is an App for That

In fact, tons of apps exist for daily habit tracking. Simply visit the app store on your smartphone and search on the topic of "habit tracking." You will find a variety of apps and many of them are free.

Download a habit tracking app that enables you to set a daily reminder that will encourage you to stop and take a few seconds to think about your commitment of 10 Minutes by Friday to try to give people more of what they CRAVE.

You will find that recognizing others for good, if not great, effort becomes more natural, almost effortless, over time. It will become ... well ... a habit! Guaranteed!

Now wait, what if you don't have a smartphone and an app store to visit? No problem. Do your tracking the old-fashioned way. Use a calendar and put an X on each day that you accomplish your goal of tracking your effort. Be like Jerry Seinfeld; try to create a streak. See how many days you can go where you take a few seconds to ask, "Did I try?"

It doesn't matter whether you are trying to make recognizing employees a habit or simply want to become a better listener. To make something habitual, you need to take a daily inventory of your thoughts, words spoken, and actions.

Habit-Building Pitfalls to Avoid

We are nearing the end of this book. You are almost ready to sprint forward and implement the Ultimate Habit, and maybe some of you will use the habit-building process to make improvements in other areas of your life. Before we wrap up, we must cover some of the pitfalls to watch out for. From years of observation, coupled with reviewing dozens of research studies on why people find it hard to stick to good habits, I've organized four common pitfalls:

1. "It's just not enjoyable."

The decision to start a new habit and make a change often feels good even before anything has changed. You've done nothing yet, but you get a warm, nice feeling. However, people often give up quickly and without as much guilt when the habit they are trying to form simply does not provide joy. When it comes to strategically recognizing employees, make sure you take the time to reflect on the benefits of providing people what they CRAVE. Think about how your efforts might make them feel. Consider your own personal feelings. And, of course, consider what business results are accelerated by the actions being recognized.

2. We are obsessed with instant gratification.

In general, we want things now rather than later. There is a psychological discomfort associated with self-denial. As humans, we are wired with a desire for instant gratification. We have the natural-born instinct to seize the rewards at hand. This is even further fueled by technology that enables us to bingewatch our favorite shows ("No way am I waiting a week to see what happens next") and order almost anything online for same-day delivery (or at least two days to your door). Want to go on a date? Swipe to the right! The possibilities for fulfilling our instant gratification are endless. In almost everything we do, we expect overnight transformation and success after one day (or a few days). When it comes to seeing and feeling the benefits of giving people what they CRAVE and witnessing accelerated business results, it takes time, often months, quarters, or even years. This is a journey that requires some patience.

3. Our goals are too lofty.

When planning to take on a habit that will be meaningful personally and/or professionally, we tend to get excited and put routines and goals in place that are simply too difficult to achieve. Ten Minutes by Friday is your goal for mastering the Ultimate Habit and it is completely achievable with a little effort. I've made this goal even more achievable by clearly stating that you don't necessarily have to document a strategic employee recognition every week (although doing so would be amazing), but that you should invest up to ten minutes weekly to stop and think about successes you've witnessed and consider a strategic recognition. One of the reasons so many leaders have found the Ultimate Habit to be so successful is because even if they only do one recognition a month, they are still doing a good job (often much better than ever before) and feel quite successful.

4. "Aw, screw this, it's not worth the effort."

The difference between the people who make habits stick and those who don't often comes down to their attitude toward slip-ups. People who fail have an all-or-nothing mentality. It's not whether you slip up, it's how you handle it that matters. The "Aw, screw it" pitfall is a close cousin to the instant gratification one noted previously. There is a scientific take on this phenomenon, called the What-the-Hell Effect, which explains why people are so likely to give up a new habit because of a slip-up. The What-the-Hell Effect describes the cycle you feel when you indulge, regret what you've done, and then go back for more. The phrase was coined by dieting researchers, but the effect can apply to any setback or willpower challenge. What happens is your brain rationalizes your behavior. For instance, suppose you are dieting and come across a plate of cookies and you eat one. Next you tell yourself, "You already blew your goal of not eating sweets, so, what the hell, you might as well eat the entire plate." According to Kelly McGonigal, who writes about the effect in *The Willpower Instinct*:

> *Giving in makes you feel bad about yourself, which motivates you to do something to feel better. And what's the cheapest, fastest strategy for feeling better? Often the very thing you feel bad about. ... It's not the first giving-in that guarantees the bigger relapse. It's the feelings of shame, guilt, loss of control and loss of hope that follow the first relapse.*[76]

Watch out for the "Aw, screw it" pitfall and What-the-Hell Effect when it comes to the Ultimate Habit. If you miss a few weeks or even a few months, don't worry about it. The most important thing is to acknowledge how you respond when you realize that you've let yourself down. Do you automatically shift into self-criticism and beat yourself up over losing control? Most people do, which only fuels the feelings of guilt or the excuses you tell yourself as to why you've not maintained your goal. The trick is to shift into a mindset of self-compassion and realize instead that what matters is consistency over time.

Consistency Over Intensity

Remember, it's all about progress, not perfection. Don't fall victim to any of the pitfalls above. If you run short on willpower or forget to demonstrate the Ultimate Habit, don't give up. What matters most is consistency over time, not the intensity of consecutive weeks. Making strategically recognizing employees truly habitual will be a process. Don't let yourself quit if you lose focus or forget. Stay committed to your daily effort tracking—a few seconds each day to ask yourself, "Did I try?" If you tried, you will make progress. Over time, you will master the Ultimate Habit of strategically recognizing employees.

Don't Wait for Someday—A Last-Minute Pep Talk

"Do-nothings" are what I call the people who learn about the Ultimate Habit, but don't actually make strategically recognizing employees habitual. Not because they didn't realize it was important or they didn't want to change. They just ran out of hours in the day. They thought they would get to it later. But "later" never came. And, therefore, nothing really changed at work regarding employee engagement, the work culture, and the customer experience. They never really got the chance to find out what the connection would be between their strategic recognition activity and the acceleration of business results. Why? Because they didn't try. They didn't encourage other leaders to try. So, people at work continued to NOT get enough of what they truly CRAVE (and deserve).

Most leadership development initiatives revolve around one tremendous false assumption that if people understand what to do then they will do it. From my experience, that's not usually true. Most of us understand; we just don't do it because it is a lot easier not to.

Up until this past year, of the thousands of people who have come to my speeches and workshops, I'm sure only a small percent followed through on what they learned and actually did something about it. But that is all changing. That is why *CRAVE* was heavily researched and packaged up for leaders like you: to give you a simple methodology and an even simpler recipe (10 Minutes by Friday) to take action on.

But why would I suggest that only a small percentage of leaders actually follow through on the change they've dreamed up right in front of me? I certainly hope it's not because I was unable to convey my message and inspire change. Here is the excuse: Even though they got excited during the initial planning of building the habit, when the dopamine release in their brains made them feel good about the positive habit-building activity they were embarking on … they eventually got back to work and began to feel as if they didn't have the time to invest in the change. It felt so good to dream it up. But, as I said earlier, this is a barrier to creating any habit. We like the initial planning phase. The dopamine release feels good. But then the dopamine wears off and the work starts. This dream takes on a narrative you may be familiar with. It goes like this:

> *I'm so busy right now. In fact, the Raging River of Responsibility is flowing fast and furious. I have too much on my mind and on my plate. My life feels somewhat out of control. I have a few unique and special challenges going on right now. But don't worry; the worst of it will be over in a couple of months. After that, I am going to take a few weeks off, get organized, spend some time with my family, eat better, and begin working out. My life will be quite a bit different then. I will be able to focus on creating the Ultimate Habit (which I know is super important). I will then begin to share it with my peers, integrate recognition sharing in my meetings, participate on our social recognition platform, and get really focused on giving people more of what they CRAVE!*

Have you ever had a dream that sounds something like this? How long have you been having this dream? Is it working for you?

Perhaps it's time to stop dreaming of a day when you won't be so busy. Because that day may never come. Your dream is an illusion! You are a high-performing individual. The Raging River of Responsibility does not stop for you. The reality is there's a good chance tomorrow will be just as crazy busy as today.

You want to be an even better, more effective, and trusted leader. If you didn't, you would never have read this book. So now is your chance to take your leadership skills to the next level by mastering the Ultimate Habit. When you do, you will get more of what you CRAVE while giving others what they CRAVE, leading to all kinds of time-saving and cost-reducing benefits that will make the Raging River of Responsibility a little bit easier to navigate. You have no excuse to wait any longer. The best time to start performing the Ultimate Habit is NOW! Ten Minutes by Friday.

Pep talk is over.

And so is this book. Thank you for joining me on the journey. Now go give someone what they CRAVE!

A Favor to Ask

Will you do me a favor?

If you feel inspired from reading *CRAVE*, if you feel motivated to help others get more of what they CRAVE, if you feel that you can become an even better leader at work, then I hope you'll do something for me.

Give this copy to someone else. Or send them a link to the book on Amazon. Ask others to read the book. Share your decision to invest 10 Minutes by Friday to help create an even better place to work.

We can all benefit when more people get their craving filled. We need more believers like you. We need you to help spread the word.

Thank you!!

APPENDIX

Google This!

Over the past decade or so, I have spent countless hours digging into the history of motivation and what humans CRAVE at work. Here are a few who inspired this book. I encourage you to Google them and learn more about the history of this topic.

1930s-1940s

- Robert Hoppock & Samuel Spiegler, "Job Satisfaction: Researches of 1935-1937" (1938)
- Abraham Maslow, "A Theory of Human Motivation" (1943)
- Richard Centers, "Motivation Aspects of Occupational Stratification" (1948)

1950s

- Harry F. Harlow, Margaret Kuenne Harlow & Donald R. Meyer, "Learning Motivated by a Manipulation Drive" (1950)
- Robert L. Kahn, "The Relationship of Productivity to Morale" (1951)
- Harry F. Harlow, "Motivation as a Factor in the Acquisition of New Responses" (1953)
- Nancy C. Morse and Robert S. Weiss, "The Function and Meaning of Work and the Job" (1955)

- Ian C. Ross and Alvin Zander, "Need Satisfactions and Employee Turnover" (1957)
- Frederick Herzberg, Bernard Mausner, and Barbara Bloch, *The Motivation to Work* (1959)

1960s

- Douglas McGregor, *The Human Side of Enterprise* (1960)
- Victor Vroom, "Ego-Involvement, Job Satisfaction, and Job Performance" (1962)
- Sam Glucksberg, "The Influence of Strength of Drive on Functional Fixedness and Perceptual Recognition" (1962)
- Daniel Katz, "The Motivational Basis of Organizational Behaviour" (1964)
- Sam Glucksberg, "Problem Solving: Response Competition Under the Influence of Drive" (1964)
- Fredrick Herzberg, "One More Time: How Do You Motivate Employees?" (1968)

1970s

- Joanne McCloskey, "Influence of Rewards and Incentives on Staff Nurse Turnover Rate" (1974)
- Ernest H. Ward, "Elements of an Employee Motivation Program" (1974)
- Edward L. Deci, *Intrinsic Motivation* (1975)
- Rabindra N. Kanungo, Sasi B. Misra, and Iswar Dayal, "Relationship of Job Involvement to Perceived Importance and Satisfaction of Employee Needs" (1975)

- Arne L. Kalleberg, "Work Values and Job Rewards: A Theory of Job Satisfaction" (1977)
- William G. Ouchi and Jerry B. Johnson, "Types of Organizational Control and Their Relationship to Emotional Well Being" (1978)

1980s

- Howard Schwartz & Stanley M. Davis, "Matching Corporate Culture and Business Strategy" (1981)
- Barry Z. Posner, James M. Kouzes & Warren H. Schmidt, "Shared Values Make a Difference: An Empirical Test of Corporate Culture" (1985)
- Edward Deci & Richard M. Ryan, *Intrinsic Motivation and Self-Determination in Human Behavior* (1985)
- Carla O'Dell and Jerry McAdams, "The Revolution in Employee Rewards" (1987)
- Lynne F. McGee, "Keeping Up the Good Work" (1988)
- John H. Bishop, "The Recognition and Reward of Employee Performance" (1989)

1990s

- Edwin A. Locke & Gary P. Latham, "Work Motivation and Satisfaction: Light at the End of the Tunnel" (1990)
- George G. Gordon & Nancy DiTomaso, "Predicting Corporate Performance from Organizational Culture" (1992)
- Bob Nelson, "Dump the Cash, Load on the Praise" (1996)
- Bruno Frey, *Not Just for the Money: An Economic Theory of Personal Motivation* (1997)

- Karen Danna & Ricky W. Griffin, "Health and Well-Being in the Workplace: A Review and Synthesis of the Literature" (1999)

2000s

- Kyle W. Luthans, "Recognition: A Powerful, but often Overlooked, Leadership Tool to Improve Employee Performance" (2000)
- Edward L. Deci & Richard M. Ryan, "Self-Determination Theory and the Facilitation of Intrinsic Motivation, Social Development, and Well-Being" (2000)
- James K. Harter, "Managerial Talent, Employee Engagement, and Business-Unit Performance" (2000)
- Michael Abrashoff, *It's Your Ship: Management Techniques from the Best Damn Ship in the Navy* (2002)
- Ron Goetzel, Ronald J. Ozminkowski, Lloyd I. Sederer & Tami L. Mark, "The Business Case for Quality Mental Health Services: Why Employers Should Care About the Mental Health and Well-Being of Their Employees" (2002)
- James K. Harter, Frank L. Schmidt & Corey L. M. Keyes, "Well-Being in the Workplace and its Relationship to Business Outcomes: A Review of the Gallup Studies" (2003)
- Paul P. Baard, Edward L. Deci, and Richard M. Ryan, "Intrinsic Need Satisfaction: A Motivational Basis of Performance and Well-Being in Two Work Settings" (2004)

- Cathy van Dyck, Michael Frese, Markus Baer & Sabine Sonnentag, "Organizational Error Management Culture and Its Impact on Performance: A Two-Study Replication" (2005)

2010s

- Ivan T. Robertson & Cary L. Cooper, "Full Engagement: The Integration of Employee Engagement and Psychological Well-Being" (2010)
- David Sturt, *Great Work: How to Make a Difference People Love* (2013)
- Octavius Black & Sebastian Bailey, *Mind Gym: Achieve More by Thinking Differently* (2014)
- Christiane Bradler, Robert Dur, Susanne Neckermann & Arjan Non, "Employee Recognition and Performance: A Field Experiment" (2016)
- Francesco Montani, Jean-Sébastien Boudrias & Marilyne Pigeon, "Employee Recognition, Meaningfulness and Behavioural Involvement: Test of a Moderated Mediation Model" (2017)

Deci and Ryan, the Story Continued ...

While I touched on Edward Deci and Richard Ryan in Part 1, I really just summarized their influence and importance. My goal was to introduce you to these pioneers and their Self-Determination Theory and show how their work inspired and ties into the theory of CRAVE. This appendix has a bit more information about their work and the hundreds of researchers and scientists who continue to apply their theories to this day.

To summarize what we covered in Part 1, the behavioral science industry has produced more than a thousand studies and associated papers that continue to point to three similar conclusions. First, you can't effectively motivate humans with control tactics (e.g., money, fear, etc.), at least not in ways that are sustainable over time. Second, the better way to motivate is to create the conditions where humans can more easily tap into their personal, intrinsic motivation. And third, the optimal way to create the environment is to enable humans to achieve their desires. As framed by Deci and Ryan in Self-Determination Theory: "If you want employees to tap into more of their personal motivation and be more committed at work, you must support an environment where employees experience the 'feelings' produced when their innate desires are met."

Rock Star Status Among the Disciples

Over the past forty years, Deci and Ryan have mentored, provided scholarships for, and inspired individuals interested in behavioral science and the study of motivation. Their efforts have produced thousands of disciples in the form of Self-Determination Theory researchers and scholars around the globe. In 1999, they held their first Self-Determination Theory conference at the University of Rochester, which turned out to be nothing more than a small meeting of presenters and students. A second conference was held in 2004 in Ottawa, and it attracted nearly two hundred participants from over thirteen countries. Inspired by the turnout, Deci and Ryan held a third conference in 2007 in Toronto, and more than three hundred practitioners from twenty-three countries convened to share research and learn about the future of Self-Determination Theory and how to apply it.

The conference after that attracted 550 researchers and practitioners; the next brought together more than six hundred from more than thirty-eight countries. In 2017, Victoria, British Columbia, hosted the largest conference yet: four days of collaboration among scientists, researchers, practitioners, and scholars; close to seven hundred from around the globe.

I sat down with Deci and Ryan on a few occasions, most recently to share the concept of *CRAVE* and how connected it is to their work. I asked them for thoughts on their theory, the relatively limited adoption by leaders in business, and what it is like to have hundreds of disciples come together to explore their theory and share their own innovative research findings.

When I asked Deci if he felt like a rock star at these conferences, he responded, "Yeah. But that is not at all what I want. Of course, it feels good to have people like us and appreciate the work we do. But rock-star status is not what Rich and I are looking for. We want to be supporting the people in the room who are using our work and are building upon it."

Next, I asked his opinion on why Self-Determination Theory is not more widely adopted in the business community. His response was as straightforward as it was obvious: "It's harder to do Self-Determination Theory than to wave money in their face. Giving people more money as a way to try and motivate is easy, but building an environment to satisfy the basic needs is damn difficult."

During our last visit together, Deci and I spent several hours discussing this book, some of his earliest research dating back to the 1960s, as well as some new research that is not yet published. I asked him what he wanted his legacy to be. His response was indicative of someone who truly wants to make the world a better place and would love to see their theory more effectively put into practice in organizations:

There are many thousands of people in the world whose lives are better because they took interest in our work on Self-Determination Theory. But most companies in North America are not using the theory, or at least they are not using it very effectively. Why? Because it is easier to use rewards and punishments than to support people's basic psychological needs for autonomy, competence, and relatedness.

I've had similar conversations with Richard Ryan. Like Deci, he shared how they love to do the work and are simply not concerned with fame or getting the credit. When I pressed Ryan on the reality that so many have taken their theory over the years and created their own (just like I've done with *CRAVE*), he responded with: "If we had tried to brand Self-Determination Theory as something we created, we would not have been able to get it out there on as large a scale. We wanted people to steal the concept and build upon it." I asked him about his personal legacy and he said he doesn't care about money or fame. Rather, "In my heart, I care about building and sharing the framework for motivation. I want to influence the change in thinking about the science of human motivation that is needed to help make the world a better place." He shared how humbling it is to attend a conference that is 100 percent based on a theory he is responsible for cultivating over the years. "The speeches provided by faculty from around the world are cool. But it's the poster sessions that get me really excited." As I learned, these poster sessions are presentations where PhD students post their Self-Determination Theory research projects, which are based on a variety of different applications in the fields of education, health care, media, and sports (among others). According to Ryan, "This is where you begin to see further evidence and new ideas on how to apply Self-Determination Theory. I feel a sense of responsibility to stay on top of the latest research and continue to support the young, talented people that are committed to building upon the theory."

Edward Deci officially retired from the University of Rochester in September 2017. He is a professor emeritus and still has an office there. He continues to travel around the world speaking, consulting, and helping others to build upon Self-Determination Theory.

Richard Ryan is a busy guy. He remains a professor at both the University of Rochester and the Institute for Positive Psychology and Education at the Australian Catholic University. In Australia, he is also heavily involved in a laboratory that does brain research in a focused attempt to understand the impact that neuropsychology—in addition to political and economic factors—has on motivation and well-being. As if that's not enough, he is also working on building the nonprofit organization he cofounded with Deci: The Center for Self-Determination Theory. Last, he also cofounded a firm with Deci and Scott Rigby called

Immersyve, which is a leading-edge research organization that also consults with businesses to help create more motivation in the workplace. You can learn more about Immersyve at www.immersyve.com.

For those of you interested in learning even more about Self-Determination Theory—and especially its application in fields outside of business—I encourage you to visit www.selfdeterminationtheory.org.

Citations

[1] Herzberg, Frederick, Bernard Mausner, and Barbara Bloch Snyderman, *The Motivation to Work* (New York: Wiley, 1959), vii.

[2] Herzberg, Frederick, Bernard Mausner, and Barbara Bloch Snyderman, *The Motivation to Work* (New York: Wiley, 1959), ix.

[3] Gallup, "State of the American Workplace," Gallup report, 2017, http://news.gallup.com/reports/199961/state-amer ican-workplace-report-2017.aspx

[4] Gallup, "State of the American Workplace," Gallup report, 2013, http://www.gallup.com/services/178517/ state-global-workplace.aspx

[5] Herzberg, Frederick, Bernard Mausner, and Barbara Bloch Snyderman, *The Motivation to Work* (New York: Wiley, 1959), 60.

[6] Herzberg, Frederick, Bernard Mausner, and Barbara Bloch Snyderman, *The Motivation to Work* (New York: Wiley, 1959), 77.

[7] O Great One! "Our Story" page, KRC Research study conducted on behalf of O Great One!, accessed March 15, 2018, https://www.whosyourogo.com/our-story

[8] O Great One! "Our Story" page, KRC Research study conducted on behalf of O Great One!, accessed March 15, 2018, https://www.whosyourogo.com/our-story

[9] O.C. Tanner, "Performance Accelerated," O.C. Tanner white paper, 2011, https://www.octanner.com/institute/white-papers/ performance-accelerated.html

[10] Globoforce, "The ROI of Social Recognitions: 7 Ways it Drives Business Success," Globoforce report, 2016, http://go.globoforce.com/rs/862-JIQ-698/images/7-Reasons-Report.pdf

[11] O.C. Tanner, "Performance Accelerated," O.C. Tanner white paper, 2011, https://www.octanner.com/institute/white-papers/performance-accelerated.html

[12] Gallup, "State of the American Workplace," Gallup report, 2017, http://news.gallup.com/reports/199961/state-amer ican-workplace-report-2017.aspx

[13] Morse, Nancy C., Robert S. Weiss, "The Function and Meaning of Work and the Job," *American Sociological Review*, no. 20 (March 1955): 198.

[14] Ross, Ian C., Alvin Zander, "Need Satisfactions and Employee Turnover," *Personnel Psychology* 10, no. 3 (Fall 1957): 327-338.

[15] Ross, Ian C., Alvin Zander, "Need Satisfactions and Employee Turnover," *Personnel Psychology* 10, no. 3 (Fall 1957): 327-338.

[16] Katz, Daniel, "The Motivational Basis of Organizational Behaviour," *Journal of Behavioural Science* 9, no. 2 (1964): 131-146.

[17] Baard, Paul P., Edward L. Deci, and Richard M. Ryan, "Intrinsic Need Satisfaction: A Motivational Basis of Performance and Well-Being in Two Work Settings," *Journal of Applied Social Psychology*, 34 (2004): 2045-2068.

[18] NSI Nursing Solutions, Inc., "2017 National Health Care Retention & RN Staffing Report," NSI Nursing Solutions, Inc., report, 2017, http://www.nsinursingsolutions.com/Files/assets/library/retention-institute/NationalHealthcareRNRetentionReport2017.pdf

[19] Dimock, Michael, "Defining generations: Where Millennials end and post-Millennials begin," Pew Research Center, March 1, 2018,

http://www.pewresearch.org/fact-tank/2018/03/01/defining-gen erations-where-millennials-end-and-post-millennials-begin/

[20] Fleming, John, "Gallup Analysis: Millennials, Marriage and Family," Gallup News, May 19, 2016, http://news.gallup.com/ poll/191462/gallup-analysis-millennials-marriage-family.aspx

[21] Fry, Richard, "Millennials surpass Gen Xers as the largest generation in U.S. labor force," Pew Research Center, May 11, 2015, http://www.pewresearch.org/fact-tank/2015/05/11/millen nials-surpass-gen-xers-as-the-largest-generation-in-u-s-labor-force/

[22] Winograd, Morley and Dr. Michael Hais, "How Millennials Could Upend Wall Street and Corporate America," Governance Studies at The Brookings Institution, May 2014, https://www.brookings.edu/ wp-content/uploads/2016/06/Brookings_Winogradfinal.pdf

[23] Gallup, "How Millennials Want to Work and Live," Gallup report, 2016, http://news.gallup.com/reports/189830/ millennials-work-live.aspx

[24] Gallup, "How Millennials Want to Work and Live," Gallup report, 2016, http://news.gallup.com/reports/189830/ millennials-work-live.aspx

[25] Kaufman, Dr. Trent, D. Joshua Christensen, and Andrew Newton, "Employee Performance: What Causes Great Work?," Cicero Group research paper, 2015, http://appreciate.octanner.com/ 2015_02_WP_DriversofGreatWork

[26] Sturt, David, Todd Nordstrom, Kevin Ames, and Gary Beckstrand, *Appreciate: Celebrating People, Inspiring Greatness*, (Salt Lake City: O.C. Tanner Institute Publishing).

[27] The Center for Generational Kinetics and Barnum Financial Group, "Unlocking Millennial Talent 2015: Brand New Insights for Employing the Fastest Growing Generation in the Workplace," The Center for Generational Kinetics white paper, 2015.

[28] Gallup, "How Millennials Want to Work and Live," Gallup report, 2016, http://news.gallup.com/reports/189830/millennials-work-live.aspx

[29] Stone, Steven, "Millennial Time Spent on Mobile Internet Gradually Increasing," News Biz Blog, posted on June 27, 2017, https://newsbizblog.org/2017/06/27/millennial-time-spent-on-mobile-internet-gradually-increasing-3/

[30] Accel + Qualtrics, "The Millennial Study," Qualtrics.com, accessed May 15, 2018, https://www.qualtrics.com/millennials/

[31] PwC, "Millennials at work: Reshaping the workplace," PwC report, 2011, https://www.pwc.de/de/prozessoptimierung/assets/millennials-at-work-2011.pdf

[32] Stillman, David and Jonah Stillman, "Move Over, Millennials; Generation Z Is Here," Society for Resource Management, posted on April 11, 2017, https://www.shrm.org/resourcesandtools/hr-topics/behavioral-competencies/global-and-cultural-effectiveness/pages/move-over-millennials-generation-z-is-here.aspx

[33] Enactus and Robert Half International Inc., "Get Ready for Generation Z," Enactus and Robert Half report, 2015.

[34] Enactus and Robert Half International Inc., "Get Ready for Generation Z," Enactus and Robert Half report, 2015.

[35] Breuning, Dr. Loretta Graziano, *Habits of a Happy Brain: Retrain Your Brain to Boost Your Serotonin, Dopamine, Oxytocin & Endorphin Levels*, (Massachusetts: Adams Media, 2016), 13.

[36] Breuning, Dr. Loretta Graziano, *Habits of a Happy Brain: Retrain Your Brain to Boost Your Serotonin, Dopamine, Oxytocin & Endorphin Levels*, (Massachusetts: Adams Media, 2016), 50.

[37] Breuning, Dr. Loretta Graziano, *Habits of a Happy Brain: Retrain Your Brain to Boost Your Serotonin, Dopamine, Oxytocin & Endorphin Levels*, (Massachusetts: Adams Media, 2016), 161.

[38] Gallup, "State of the American Workplace," Gallup report, 2017, http://news.gallup.com/reports/199961/state-amer ican-workplace-report-2017.aspx

[39] Eisenberger, Robert, Glenn P. Malone, and William D. Presson, "Optimizing Perceived Organizational Support to Enhance Employee Engagement," Society for Human Resource Management and Society for Industrial and Organizational Psychology, 2016.

[40] Globoforce, "The ROI of Recognition in Building a More Human Workplace," WorkHuman Research Institute report, 2016.

[41] Gallup, "State of the American Workplace," Gallup report, 2017, http://news.gallup.com/reports/199961/state-amer ican-workplace-report-2017.aspx

[42] Bob Chapman, quoted by Annette Franz, "We Have a Crisis of Leadership," CX Journey, posted November 8, 2017, http://www.cx-journey.com/2017/11/ we-have-crisis-in-leadership.html

[43] Smith, Steve, "A Category at a Crossroads," presented at business planning session with Starr Conspiracy, August 23, 2017.

[44] Gallup, "State of the American Manager: Analytics and Advice for Leaders," Gallup report, 2015, http://www.gallup.com/ services/182138/state-american-manager.aspx

[45] Gallup, "State of the American Manager: Analytics and Advice for Leaders," Gallup report, 2015, http://www.gallup.com/ services/182138/state-american-manager.aspx

[46] Gallup, "State of the American Manager: Analytics and Advice for Leaders," Gallup report, 2015, http://www.gallup.com/ services/182138/state-american-manager.aspx

[47] O.C. Tanner, "Influencing Greatness: Giving, Receiving, and Observing Recognition," O.C. Tanner white paper, 2016,

https://www.octanner.com/institute/white-papers.html

[48] Rogers, Everett M., *Diffusion of Innovations*, (New York, The Free Press: 1995), 4.

[49] Sutton, Robert, *Good Boss, Bad Boss: How to Be the Best… and Learn from the Worst*, (New York, Business Plus: 2010).

[50] Google; Google Dictionary; "Definition of Stress"

[51] EKU Online, "Work Related Stress on Employees Health," info-graphic, https://safetymanagement.eku.edu/resources/infographics/work-related-stress-on-employees-health/

[52] Quoted by Maeghan Ouimet, "The Real Productivity-Killer: Jerks," Inc.com, posted November 15, 2012, https://www.inc.com/maeghan-ouimet/real-cost-bad-bosses.html

[53] McQuaid, Michelle quoted by Jack Zenger, "New Research: To Reach Full Work Potential, Hone In On Your Strengths," Forbes.com, posted March 6, 2015, https://www.forbes.com/sites/jackzenger/2015/03/06/new-research-to-reach-full-work-potential-hone-in-on-your-strengths/

[54] Murhpy, Lawrence R. and Theodore F. Schoenborn, "Stress Management in Work Settings," Centers for Disease Control and Prevention, 1987, https://www.cdc.gov/niosh/docs/87-111/

[55] Nyberg, A., L. Alfredsson, T. Theorell, H. Weserlund, J. Vahtera, and M. Kivimäki, "Managerial Leadership and Ischaemic Heart Disease Among Employees: The Swedish WOLF Study," *Journal of Occupational and Environmental Medicine* 66, no. 1 (2009): 51-55, doi:10.1136/oem.2008.039.

[56] O.C. Tanner, "Performance Accelerated," O.C. Tanner white paper, 2011, https://www.octanner.com/institute/white-papers/performance-accelerated.html

57 Goldsmith, Marshall, Speech given at leadership event for Fast Tracking Leaders, Rochester, New York, March 26, 2012.

58 Goldsmith, Marshall, "Have the Courage to Ask," Leader to Leader Institute article, posted May 2, 2005, http://www.marshallgoldsmith.com/articles/have-the-courage-to-ask/

59 Hyken, Shep, "Bad Customer Service Costs Businesses Billions Of Dollars," *Forbes* online, posted August 27, 2016, https://www.forbes.com/sites/shephyken/2016/08/27/bad-customer-service-costs-businesses-billions-of-dollars/#73edfde05152

60 New Voice Media, "The $62 Billion Customer Service Scared Away," New Voice Media article, posted May 23, 2016, https://www.newvoicemedia.com/en-us/news/the-62-billion-customer-service-scared-away

61 Quiring, Kevin, Fabio De Angelis, and Esther Gasull, "Digital Disconnect in Customer Engagement," Accenture.com article, https://www.accenture.com/us-en/insight-digital-disconnect-customer-engagement

62 New Voice Media, "The $62 Billion Customer Service Scared Away," New Voice Media article, posted May 23, 2016, https://www.newvoicemedia.com/en-us/news/the-62-billion-customer-service-scared-away

63 Hyken, Shep, "Bad Customer Service Costs Businesses Billions Of Dollars," *Forbes* online, posted August 27, 2016, https://www.forbes.com/sites/shephyken/2016/08/27/bad-customer-service-costs-businesses-billions-of-dollars/#73edfde05152

64 Quoted by Laura Fagan, "Customer Service Stats: 55% of Consumers Would Pay More for a Better Service Experience," Salesforce.com blog, posted October 24, 2013, https://www.salesforce.com/blog/2013/10/customer-service-stats-55-of-consumers-would-pay-more-for-a-better-service-experience.html

[65] Quoted by Laura Fagan, "Customer Service Stats: 55% of Consumers Would Pay More for a Better Service Experience," Salesforce.com blog, posted October 24, 2013, https://www.salesforce.com/blog/2013/10/customer-ser vice-stats-55-of-consumers-would-pay-more-for-a-bet ter-service-experience.html

[66] Hyken, Shep, "Bad Customer Service Costs Businesses Billions Of Dollars," *Forbes* online, posted August 27, 2016, https://www.forbes.com/sites/shephyken/2016/08/27/bad-cus tomer-service-costs-businesses-billions-of-dollars/#73edfde05152

[67] Fine, Cordelia, *A Mind of Its Own: How Your Brain Distorts and Deceives*, (New York, W.W. Norton & Company: 2006), 8.

[68] Statistic Brain Institute, "New Years Resolution Statistics," Statistic Brain Research Institute online, posted January 9, 2018, https://www.statisticbrain.com/new-years-resolution-statistics/

[69] Luciani, Joseph, "Why 80 Percent of New Year's Resolutions Fail," U.S. News & World Report online, posted December 29, 2015, https://health.usnews.com/health-news/blogs/eat-run/ articles/2015-12-29/why-80-percent-of-new-years-resolutions-fail

[70] Timeanddate.com, "Fun Holiday — Ditch New Year's Resolution Day," https://www.timeanddate.com/holidays/fun/ ditch-new-years-resolution-day

[71] Polivy, Janet, "The False Hope Syndrome: Unrealistic Expectations of Self-Change," *International Journal of Obesity* 25, Suppl 1 (2001), doi:10.1038/sj.ijo.0801705.

[72] Deutschman, Alan, "Change or Die," *Fast Company* online, posted May 1, 2005, https://www.fastcompany.com/52717/change-or-die

[73] Williams, David K., "Exceptional Leaders Create An Awareness of Greatness In The Workplace," *Forbes* online, posted September 23, 2015, https://www.forbes.com/sites/davidkwilliams/2015/

09/23/exceptional-leaders-create-an-awareness-of-great
ness-in-the-workplace/#74c63c64227f

74 Neal, David T., Wendy Wood, and Jeffrey M. Quinn, "Habits—A
Repeat Performance," Duke University, 2006,
https://dornsife.usc.edu/assets/sites/208/docs/
Neal.Wood.Quinn.2006.pdf

75 Norcross, John C. and Dominic J. Vangarelli, "The Resolution Solution: Longitudinal Examination of New Year's Change Attempts,"
Journal of Substance Abuse 1, no. 2 (1988-1989), 127-134,
https://doi.org/10.1016/S0899-3289(88)80016-6

76 McGonigal, Kelly, *The Willpower Instinct: How Self-Control Works,
Why It Matters, and What You Can Do To Get More Of It*, (New York,
Penguin Group: 2012).